GROWING
THROUGH
PERSONAL
CRISIS

EDGAR CAYCE'S WISDOM FOR THE NEW AGE

General Editor: Charles Thomas Cayce
Project Editor: A. Robert Smith

_____

Dreams: Tonight's Answers for Tomorrow's Questions,
  Mark Thurston

Awakening Your Psychic Powers, Henry Reed

Reincarnation: Claiming Your Past, Creating Your Future,
  Lynn Elwell Sparrow

Healing Miracles: Using Your Body Energies,
  William A. McGarey, M.D.

Mysteries of Atlantis Revisited, Edgar Evans Cayce, Gail Cayce
  Schwartzer, and Douglas G. Richards

Growing Through Personal Crisis, Harmon Hartzell Bro with June
  Avis Bro

Other books by Harmon Hartzell Bro

Begin a New Life

Edgar Cayce on Dreams

Edgar Cayce on Religion and Psychic Experience

High Play

Paradoxes of Rebirth

Dream Resources: A Guide (with June Avis Bro)

GROWING THROUGH PERSONAL CRISIS

HARMON HARTZELL BRO, Ph.D.
with JUNE AVIS BRO, D.Min.

1817

Harper & Row, Publishers, San Francisco

Cambridge, Hagerstown, New York, Philadelphia, Washington
London, Mexico City, São Paulo, Singapore, Sydney

Excerpt from "A Sleep of Prisoners" from *Three Plays* by Christopher Fry used with permission of Oxford University Press.

The authors gratefully acknowledge the aid of Mr. Kim Lee of Langley, Washington in creating the index.

FIRST EDITION

Library of Congress Cataloging-in-Publication Data
Bro, Harmon Hartzell, 1919–
   Growing through personal crisis.

   Bibliography: p.
   1. Life change events—Psychological aspects.
2. Adjustment (Psychology)   3. Self-Actualization (Psychology)   4. Cayce, Edgar, 1877–1945.   I. Bro, June Avis.   II. Title.
BF637.L53B76   1988   131   88-45127
ISBN 0-06-250101-1 (pbk.)

88   89   90   91   92   FG   10 9 8 7 6 5 4 3 2 1

CONTENTS

**PART TWO: THE PRACTICE OF GROWING
THROUGH PERSONAL CRISIS   151**

FOREWORD

"It is a time in the earth when people everywhere seek to know more of the mysteries of the mind, the soul," said my grandfather, Edgar Cayce, from an unconscious trance from which he demonstrated a remarkable gift for clairvoyance.

His words are prophetic even today, as more and more Americans in these unsettled times are turning to psychic explanations for daily events. For example, according to a national survey by the National Opinion Research Council nearly half of American adults today believe they have been in contact with someone who has died, a figure twice that of ten years ago. Two-thirds of all adults say they have had an ESP experience; ten years ago that figure was only one-half.

Every culture throughout history has made note of its own members' gifted powers beyond the five senses. These rare individuals held special interest because they seemed able to provide solutions to life's pressing problems. And America in the twentieth century is no exception.

Edgar Cayce was perhaps the most famous and most carefully documented psychic of our time. He began to use his unusual abilities when he was a young man, and from then on for over 40 years he would, usually twice a day, lie on a couch, go into a sleeplike state, and respond to questions. Over 14,000 of these discourses, called readings, were carefully transcribed by his secretary and preserved by the Edgar Cayce Foundation in Virginia Beach, Virginia. These psychic readings continue to provide inspiration, insight, and physical help to tens of thousands of people.

Having only an eighth-grade education, Edgar Cayce lived a plain, simple life by the world's standards. As early as childhood in Hopkinsville, Kentucky, however, he sensed that he had psychic ability. While alone he had a vision of a woman who told him he would have unusual abilities to help people. Other times he related experiences of "seeing" dead relatives. Once, while struggling with school lessons, he slept on his spelling book and awakened knowing the entire contents of the book.

As a young man he experimented with hypnosis to treat his own recurring throat problem that caused him to lose his speech. He discovered that under hypnosis he could diagnose and describe treatments for the physical ailments of others, often without knowing or seeing the person with the ailment. People began to ask him other sorts of questions and he found himself able to answer these as well.

In 1910 the *New York Times* published a two-page story with pictures about Edgar Cayce's psychic ability as described by a young physician, Wesley Ketchum, to a clinical research society in Boston. From that time on people from all over the country with every conceivable question sought his help.

In addition to his unusual talents, Cayce was a deeply religious man who taught Sunday School all of his adult life and read the entire Bible once for every year that he lived. He always tried to attune himself to God's will by studying the Scriptures and maintaining a rich prayer life, as well as by trying to be of service to those who came seeking help. He used his talents only for helpful purposes. Cayce's simplicity and humility and his commitment to doing good in the world continues to attract people to the story of his life and work and to the far-reaching information he gave.

In this series we hope to provide the reader with insights in the search for understanding and meaning in life. Each book in the series explores its subject from the viewpoint of the Edgar Cayce readings and compares perspectives of other metaphysical literature and of current scientific thought. The interested reader needs no prior knowledge of the Edgar Cayce information. When one of the Edgar Cayce readings is quoted, the identifying number of that reading is included for those who may wish to read the full text. Each volume includes suggestions for further study.

For this book, *Growing Through Personal Crisis*, authors Harmon and June Bro are exceptionally well qualified. First, they knew and worked with Edgar Cayce during the last years of his life and thus gained a deep understanding of his special approach and philosophy. Since then they have enjoyed long careers as ministers and counselors helping countless people cope with the trials of personal crisis, and as lecturers on personal spiritual development.

Their fine book can help anyone who wants not only to survive today's crisis but to grow and gain strength for dealing with those that tomorrow may bring.

Charles Thomas Cayce

Introduction

IN HIS VERSE PLAY *A Sleep of Prisoners*, Christopher Fry creates a
powerful closing scene that takes up the theme of growing through
personal crisis. Four soldiers in an unknown war are prisoners, quar-
tered in a church. They sleep fitfully, dreaming episodes both biblical
and personal, while talking and walking in their sleep. Their dreams
mirror the actual dynamics of the prisoners: violence, indifference,
competitiveness, dependency, and more. Yet the dreams also suggest
human nobility trying to get loose and find full expression.

The weary battlers suffer deeply. One soldier dreams he is Adam,
watching one of his sons kill his brother. Another soldier, as Abra-
ham, nearly slays his young son, Isaac. Absalom dies while trying to
take the kingdom away from his father, David. Finally three of the
soldiers dream they are Shadrac, Meshac, and Abednego, tied up and
thrown by King Nebuchadnezzar into a fiery furnace. To their aston-
ishment, they do not die, but discover instead that the flames have
only burned off their ropes and set them free.

As the drama closes, they all awaken from a "sleep of prisoners,"
which suggests the condition of us all: when we are groggy with our
fears and pain, and besotted with habit, we miss what the universe is
trying to nurture in us.

Who escapes confronting panic or stupefying loss? In adult life, relationships are torn apart, career and income crumble, and noble causes dissolve. We bump into our own limitations: addiction tangles our lives, our passions outstrip our commitments, age delivers its unwelcome message that we are no longer who we thought. Is there indeed a way to grow through frightening personal crises, a way that can help the fires of pain set us free to embrace life?

The life, gift, and ideas of Edgar Cayce can show us how to find our own way out of the flames. Cayce struggled with many crises. The resources he drew on in his own life, and which he shared with others through thousands of "readings," provide us with a set of values and methods we can use to grow successfully through personal crisis.

THE THREE RESPONSES TO CRISIS: COPING, CREATING, TRANSFORMING

This book is about three human responses to crisis: coping, creating, and transforming. Each is a stage in the process of growing through personal crisis, yet each may overlap the others.

Coping comes first. Even in crisis, we have to go on with life: eating, hoping to sleep, trying to talk with people, paying the bills, filling our posts, seeking places for our anger, guilt, and fear of losing control. Most crises involve some form of loss—a lost relationship, a lost opportunity, a loss of trust. In the most severe losses, we have all we can do just to keep on. We can hardly believe how others go right on behaving as though the world has not ended. The challenge is simply to manage with some dignity and grace, while the mouth dries up with anxiety. Chapter one is about the coping response.

The second response to crisis is not always available until weeks or months have passed. It is *creating*, finding new solutions. Not every problem can be restructured or reenvisioned in such a way that we can draw on the adrenaline of despair to throw us into a new activity that is rewarding to us and helpful to others. But there are times during crisis when we can be inventive or can plan and cultivate new relationships in order to try to solve the stupefying challenges of our lives. Chapter two discusses a basic process of deep growth that helps us respond to any major challenge. Chapters three, four, and five consider leads from Edgar Cayce for fashioning fresh solutions, by inspiration and creativity that reach past self-doubt.

The third response to crisis, *transforming*, comes when the darkest days and nights have passed. Sometimes we seem wakened by crisis to new maturity, new commitments, new talents, new faith, in such measure that everyone close to us knows we are taller than before. From our fiery furnace we step forward to freedom that does not reckon by pain, but by presence—being fully there for others, and able to stand firm where we so often fell before. Chapter two describes a generic process of deep growth that includes enlarging personhood; and chapter six will consider Cayce's view of karma stretching our selfhood, even while we may question God's love in our time of desperation.

The chapters in Part II consider ways we can begin to deal with particular kinds of crises. These are based on perspectives from Edgar Cayce's counsel and viewed in the light of his life and gift. We will look at crises of the heart, crises of work and social problems, and crises of colliding with ourselves.

PART I

The Art of Growing
Through Personal Crisis

1

When Coping Is Everything

EDGAR CAYCE (1877–1945) often dealt with the flames of crisis in his extraordinary life. As a healthy young teenager, busy on a Kentucky farm, he developed an astonishing ability to memorize sections of any book he chose by reading them, praying, and sleeping on them. A well-meaning country doctor, with whose daughter Cayce was enamored, told him that his strange ability to memorize meant he could never marry or have children, and would die insane. The lad worried about this prediction for years.

When Cayce was a young man selling insurance and stationery supplies in small Kentucky towns, he lost his voice for a year. Medical experts from as far away as Europe told him the handicap would be permanent. Despairing, he became a photographer's assistant, expecting to spend his life silently developing prints in darkrooms. He later ran a series of his own photographic studios, only to have them burn three times, and once force him into humiliating bankruptcy. Eventually he paid off all his creditors, but came out with nothing to show for several years of his intensive labors.

Despite his youthful fears, Cayce did marry. His family crises were far worse than his business setbacks: the Cayces had one child who died shortly after birth; another child was almost blinded by an explosion of photographic flash powder; and Cayce's vivacious wife nearly died of tuberculosis.

Cayce's voice was restored by an unusual combination of hypnosis and prayer. With his voice, however, came another crisis: he developed unusual gifts as a seer. Cayce had little on which to model the use of this gift. For several years, he used the ability to help cure the physically ill—without charge. Eventually, against his better judgment, he tried to use it for profit—to predict the outcome of wheat markets and horse races—and lost his gift entirely. He thought it had been permanently destroyed by his lack of integrity about its spiritual origins and purpose. When it returned, after a year, Cayce's unusual ability continued to serve him well on thousands of medical cases, but failed repeatedly on a venture to make money from oil drilling (which he had undertaken to finance a hospital for his work). Eventually he got the hospital from other sponsorship, and a promising new university as well, but lost them both when the pressures of the Great Depression added to conflicts among his idealistic backers. In addition, while giving his life-rescuing medical readings away from home, he was twice briefly jailed and humiliated. Crises were as familiar to him as relatives.

Cayce struggled all through his adult years with the crisis-fraught riddle of helping others by way of a process which he himself never saw or heard, never fully understood, and which he knew might be dangerous. Professionals often doubted his truthfulness and even his sanity, though no competent and thorough investigator—and there were a number—ever charged him with fraud or triviality. Along with these daunting external challenges, he also struggled with internal conflicts of tendencies to go to extremes, self-doubt, strong emotions, and loneliness. His strange calling brought him appreciation and even dangerous adulation; but it often kept others at arm's length, wondering what unwelcome features he might see in them. When his published biography brought him a measure of recognition in his later years, it also brought him thousands upon thousands of requests for emergency aid. During a wartime period that demanded sacrifices of everyone, his earnest effort to assist these sufferers wore him out and cost him his life.

The fact that Edgar Cayce had a difficult and unusual life does not in itself qualify him as a helpful source on the art of growing through crises. But insofar as he tried to live what he saw during his unusual trance vision, and to live what he taught all his life in Bible classes in mainstream churches, his own efforts add depth and authenticity to his counsel. Those of us who knew him well have no doubt that he tried to practice the principles he espoused, even though he had the kind of mixed success and failure that most of us do. It is also likely that his own heartbreaks helped to sensitize him at the deep, unconscious level his trance counsel engaged, so that his aid was as compassionate as it was inspired.

WHEN COPING IS EVERYTHING

Not every problem is a crisis. Some critical moments are just times for decision, tough but necessary. For example, a skilled saleswoman for computer software, who knows her customers and her products, may be given a week—one of the longest in her life—to decide whether to take the post offered to her as sales manager. This is a pressure-filled challenge, but it is not crippling.

Sometimes we are faced with the agony of acknowledging a chronic problem. Perhaps our miserable childhood finally stands trembling before us, stripped bare by psychotherapy or by our infantile behavior, and we must walk up to it and embrace it. Perhaps financial hardship has made us mean-spirited, so that now we must call up quiet heroism to dance again, even in the dust of beaten-down dreams. These are difficult times, but they are not the jolting shocks of real crises.

Coping becomes everything when the blow comes out of nowhere and hits us right in the face. For example, you may be struck forcefully after you have succeeded in believing that the thing you fear won't really happen: your mother must be permanently placed in the nursing home against her will; your younger brother, alternately winsome and sullen, takes his life; your company folds, and all your retirement benefits go down the tube; you discover you have a terminal illness.

In all such deadly doings, the first—and only—thing to do is simply to cope. You just need to get by. As pastoral counselors and psychotherapists, we have helped many hundreds of people deal with crises for a combined total of over sixty years. For us, experience—supported by research—has suggested some rules of thumb about the length of time it takes to recover from personal calamities.

A major crisis requires three or four months just to get past the craziness of self-blame, emotional vulnerability, and the craving to cut deals with life on terms cheaper than it is for sale. Once that first period is over, we tell our clients or constituents not to expect to claim their new selfhood—a selfhood that may have a permanent, but not necessarily disabling hole in it—in any less time than it takes to generate a newborn: namely, nine months.

As in a pregnancy, the body must process a crisis. Glands have to secrete in new ways; nerves and muscles must carry shifted loads of responsibility; senses must ease up on involuntary vigil; gut and groin must adjust to different kinds and degrees of appetites. In fact, a year and part of the next, with the full round of seasons, is not too long just to spend coping. As the earth changes, we can see our slow growth through crisis reflected in hundreds of primal human images: the slow parade of weather, the blooming and wilting of plants, the spawning and roaming of creatures. Social rituals hold to other rhythms and images that carry and renew us—elections, business conventions, shopping, family holidays, weddings and funerals, sports and picnics.

When the shock of a crisis still seems to disembowel us regularly after two years, we may reasonably look to see whether one event may be masking another and deeper loss. For example, a competent woman among our clients mourned overlong the death of her hydrocephalic daughter, whose survival chances she knew were severely limited. With help, she discovered that the real unresolved dying lay in her foundering marriage to an alcoholic husband.

Certain factors can make the coping go faster or slower. The *manner* of a blow can spear us deeply. The death of a child in a violent auto accident takes more out of us than the death of a youngster by infection, because of the brutal force. The *centrality* of a loss in our lives makes a difference to recovery. To a workaholic, for example, a smashed career may be far more costly emotionally than a mastectomy.

Having real *helpers* among dear and wise friends and relatives, or among professionals—who are a kind of temporary relative—can cut the desperate time by a third or more. Getting to process a loss *in advance*, as we can when a loved one is terminally ill, can make the coping go more swiftly than handling sudden tragedy. *Too many* crises at once can do in even the stoutest heart and frame. The way we *generally cope* with frustrations is heightened during debilitating crises: do we cope by blaming others or indulging in grief, or by taking aim and action? Our *dependency* style—whether we are able to lean on others for support, or whether we destructively live through others—is also a factor. Having a *personal lore* of crises and their navigation makes a positive difference—this may be tales of relatives who survived hardship, great films, myths and legends, or even wise fairy tales of hardship transcended.

Finally our experience suggests, as Cayce often pointed out, that an active *shared faith*—a spiritual path in community, not just holding to dogma or abiding by rituals and codes—can cut the blind suffering by as much as half. Such faith, however, must not be used simply to deny the pain, the absurdity, or the loneliness of a bitter crisis.

TRUSTING THE BODY

The body has its own wisdom and ways when set upon by crisis. Cayce's counsel to people in severe distress almost always began with gentle care for the flesh as a basis for all other coping. As our nearest of kin, the body deserves our attention and respect. It is our closest companion, who has been with us everywhere and done everything we have. During severe crisis, it shuts down to mere operating, using intermittent hibernation while it consults with the mind and spirit on new directions.

The body offers sleep, the cheapest and often the safest tranquilizer. We are amazed how tired and stupefied we are, just wanting to sit or lie still and forget phones and well-wishers. The fatigue deserves patient respect, for weeks or several months. But bodies differ. Some of us crave action as much as rest, to handle the adrenaline of distress. We may chop a stack of wood, reorganize a shop, or tear into housecleaning before we settle down to incubation.

Some bodies in despair want desperately to pump happy chemicals through the system, and may cry out for sex or food. Most of us sleep only fitfully and stare into the nightly dark for several months. When we are truly shaken, the body may surprise us with new aches and pains, with trembling, or with inability to concentrate or remember familiar skills and phone numbers. We may plummet back into forgotten times, happier than the present—as when Willy Loman in *Death of a Salesman* tries fruitlessly to open the windshield of his car as he once did in a long-ago auto for soothing rides through the country.

The body helps out with the biochemistry of denial, supplying hallucinations, or the momentary certainty that the awful event did not happen. It may also refuse to go near threatening scenes or unbearable reminders. Yet the body must be desensitized to threat, so that its alarms can slowly be turned off and so that it may return to the daily routine. So it will keep running over terrible details selectively, or performing meaningless little rituals, or taking us back to particular places, until it gets the needed signals that the world is safe again. For the same purpose, it gives us recurrent nightmares, uncovers moods we didn't know were in us, or didn't know were so close to the surface: rage, jealousy, sudden alternations between tranquility and tears, not wanting to live, passionately loving and fearing God at the same time. Like a traveling actor suddenly called upon to play unknown roles, it unpacks all our trunks and tries on strange outfits, to find one that works.

Common human experience carries much wisdom about befriending the body during this coping period. Cayce's trance aid echoed and amplified this judgment. Giving in to sleep helps; eating helps; and medication may help in the short term, but not when it is taken for so long that it dulls us to the voice of our pain. Alcohol offers its aid at the price of making us doubt our control, and disturbing our nightly ninety-minute sleep/dream cycles—just when we need dream help. Surprisingly, keeping up routines helps stabilize the body after shock leaves. We need to stay busy at ordinary work and walks, at play and housekeeping, even though we may tire easily for quite some weeks.

We need to get dressed, and look a little special in clothes we like, even when we are tempted to appear as seedy as we feel. Talking with those who understand—and don't claim to understand too much—can reassure the body with calm and loving tones. Our own flesh behaves much like a frightened pet, responding to tone of voice even when it doesn't understand the words. As Cayce often reminded sufferers, the body remembers and welcomes the good feelings that come when we help others in small but genuine ways, with a smile we'd almost forgotten was in us. There is healing in doing the dishes, rocking the baby, feeding the cat, rubbing someone's back, getting the mail, putting away tools, repairing a loose stairstep, filing stacked forms for a harried coworker.

When life clobbers us, the body deserves the extra little attentions that in other times might get skipped. A sort of chivalry applies, as we salute this intimate companion who must make the pilgrimage through the dark valley with us, sometimes going ahead of us by its own native wisdom. Loved music bypasses the mind to comfort and realign our very cells. Warm baths and prized desserts help. So do our best underwear and nightclothes, our loveliest jewelry, and outfits that boldly stand off the weather. Particular colors, in cloth and glass or flowers and candles, can be arranged around us with surprisingly direct responses from the flesh. For many, masturbation is not outrageous, though unhurried intercourse offers the whole dance. The body can hug others well when the mind forgets what to say. It keeps available the secret way of tears that can dissolve even the granite of impenetrable events.

WORKING WITH THE MIND

The body's wisdom is mute, but the mind in crisis seems never to shut up. Crisis agitates the psyche, until we fear we may never think straight again. We can help the mind to heal when it is overwhelmed, but first we must understand how it works.

To begin with, the mind is layered, as most of us recognize when we discriminate between its conscious and unconscious realms. Cayce regularly contrasted the workings of levels of the mind, noting that the drives and appetites of the "body mind" are different from the ruminations and schemes of the "mental mind," as well as from the inspiration and peace of the "soul mind." Even if we do not use such categories, we can all recognize that conflicting currents tumble and push through our thoughts in times of harsh circumstances.

Anxiety

Part of the mind, linked to primal drives and instinctual reflexes, will snuggle up to the flesh in crisis, looking for signals placed there from time immemorial, since cave bears stole the screaming children. It will post guards to watch for more bears, and stay truly anxious for a time, even when others tell us things are under control. It will jolt us awake in panic, although just a short while ago it blessed us with slumber. It will overreact to bills, and to gadgets or equipment that break down. It will worry that others may not do what they promised. It will keep even the most open-hearted people preoccupied with themselves and their need for privacy, as it should. It will remind us that we do not know how deep the caves of crisis are until we have had time to feel them out and determine where the rocks for future bear attacks are stacked.

Denial

At the same time, another part of the mind linked to the conscience or superego will be setting up to run classes in regret and guilt as a course in "great lessons in life." Dreams may actually show us in classrooms or admonished by impressive figures. The task of the conscience is to ensure that we do not repeat any dumb mistakes, but instead operate with approved standards and strategies. First it will shut the doorway to reality in moments of denial, enabling us simply to breathe and go to the bathroom without falling apart. We will keep thinking there has been some mistake, that God will take over and make things right, that we can't be as vulnerable as we feel, and that what we don't mention will evaporate by its own stupid dynamics. It will make us grab others to be sure they haven't disappeared, and offer us moments of calm that impress us—until we discover that the price has been denying what we can't get around.

Rage

Right along with brief respites through denial will come deliveries of emotional TNT, as though to help us blow away the absurd circumstances with rage or cutting remarks. Nobody is spared burning anger in serious crisis, although some hide it quickly and others ride it out. Not to be angry at loss, even the loss of intangible hopes and hidden self-respect—let alone the loss of a uniquely precious relationship—would mean we were mere bystanders in our lives. And that way lies madness, where we invent a magic world and move into it.

Catharsis is a necessary part of grief, as the Greeks understood when they presented their harsh tragedies in open amphitheaters under the unwearying stars. We feel that somebody, something must pay or hurt in proportion to the violation we experience; the outrage demands that we rage out. Lovers or relatives may be astounded at the force of our outburst, as we may also. But penetrating insights about our lives are ever escorted by warriors, who understand the flash of the moment of truth in hot strife. Priests come later, turning raw insight into tempered wisdom. Each of us must find a way to ride out the fury, without compounding our despair by mindlessly wounding others.

Sooner or later, we come to accuse and storm at God, however named. This, too, is necessary. Those who too quickly require that we stifle the ultimate anger at the Creator of all this mess serve us poorly—as did Job's talkative, rationalizing friends, who offended the One they justified. Big answers require big questions, and big personhood requires being able to rage at the whirlwind, until it finally calls us by name.

Self-blame

What we *cannot* afford is to rage overlong at ourselves, as Cayce consistently advised. Part of the mind will relentlessly review all the mistakes we made that might have led to the crisis, making sure that the present trauma brings up everything like it from the past. The job of this realm of the psyche is to learn from blows and to teach. It will do this with ruthless determination and obsessive self-blaming unless tempered by kind words, usually best received from someone other than ourselves. Certainly we will not be forgiven our neglects and excesses—and who does not have them?—if we try to swagger our way through crisis. All of us have matters to regret, knots to undo, and restitutions to make. But the rage that is supposed to scare off bears as an instinctual defense, and to lead us through catharsis to demanding an accounting from God will cripple us if we turn it full blast and unremittingly on ourselves as self-blame. Self-attack is the one assault we cannot easily repel, because the marauder is already inside our gates.

Coping requires gentleness with ourselves, even in drastic circumstances. Inner instruction in self-improvement needs to be brief, with plenty of recesses and frequent commencements, but no pompous addresses. As we shall see in the Cayce worldview that includes karma, the soul has its ways of learning from suffering, by deep inner comparisons not at once clear to the surface mind. As the ancient tale of the Garden of Eden warns, the fruit of the tree of knowing good and evil is dangerous for mortals who judge blame too easily.

Despair

The bleakness of loss makes us vulnerable to real depression rather than useful grieving and leave-taking. What tips sadness into hollow meaninglessness may be utter fatigue. But it may also be self-attack, rather than honest doubt. Doubt cleans up the room where we stand, until the spare setting lets some light splash on us. Asking "Why me?" is fair and fruitful, even if it draws no bolts of understanding from Jove. But asking "What if?" or trying on another "If only" can undo us, because it arrogates to us omnipotence over events, which we do not really have.

In despair, guilt can be murderous. Thoughts come unbidden of the easiest murder: suicide. We have moments of surprising jealousy of people who went untouched and unnoticing in our loss. We may even find ourselves secretly rejoicing at those who also suffer, or will yet suffer, just to affirm our worth. But gently holding the hand of our own sadness will lead us past all this, even though it requires the pain of having everything we see or do remind us, for a time, of our loss or blow. Apparently we are marvelously made, such that honest feelings cannot easily undo us, while posing or pretending can.

Imagination. The part of the mind that imagines is not sleeping while all this denying and raging, doubting and weeping, is going on. The imagination, like a fairy darting from blossom to blossom, is busy idealizing the lover we lost, the job that should have been ours, the innocence we would like to reclaim. It spins a gossamer cloak of possibilities to get us moving again. Sometimes it develops whole scenarios of what might have happened, had things been a little different. But we need to tell it to get on toward new directions, not paint the wilted flowers.

The lively imagination can serve us well if we ask it to take hands with memory in a different way, reminding us of all that is worthy of true gratitude, despite our loss. Here it can shine, especially when others enter into the celebration, and recreate scenes that astonish the wounded heart with fair sunniness. Grief can even spring the lock on humor, to our surprise, as imagination clasps the ridiculous memory and makes us tell it out loud, even if we must cry through our laughter.

Stabilizing the Mind

The common wisdom of human folk knows much about helping the mind in crisis. Cayce's counsel to traumatized people highlighted just such procedures. Schedules and routines can help to stabilize the ever-running computer of thought and its whizzing screens of emotions. Meals and hikes, bedtimes and worship, shopping and chores, daily work and reading the paper—these do not merely get our mind off our troubles, they get back an errant mind to handle those very troubles. Physical activity helps the besieged mind, once we are past the desperate weariness. Washing laundry and dishes, chasing kids or the dog, carrying cartons at work, may stabilize the mind by synchronizing it with muscles that still function, and with senses that still know what to see and hear and touch that matters, even when the world is obviously never going to be the same again.

Nature offers great gifts to the wounded psyche, as Cayce consistently reminded those disoriented by pain. It brims with tides that come and go, moons that blossom and wither, winds that blow and die down, seasons that follow seasons. All things growing proclaim cycles of setting forth and returning, death and rebirth. In nature, endings lead straight into beginnings—as they never do in appliances that break or cars that simply wear out. But nature keeps the ways of the eternal, as well, in unyielding mountains, unwearying waterfalls, unending sea horizons. The mind that reels can take its bearings by these and the night stars, just as it can by lovely sunlight that warms a tired and grieving body.

Every culture provides for alternation of solitude and talk during times of crisis. Cayce gave careful attention to both. The hush of cathedrals and the stillness of fishing or gardening are matched by gatherings of the clan and friends, where rites stitch up the torn fabric of existence that nobody can mend alone. And the wise old man or woman, the seasoned elder, waits to be consulted, or just to listen to words the wounded must speak lest they implode with sadness. Sometimes the precious discourse must be done with strangers, vested with tribal dignity and charged to care; such people, in our times, are called mental health professionals. Sometimes the words must tumble out before strangers in a group—single parents or Alzheimer relatives, fellow sufferers recovering from alcohol or gambling or overeating. The mind believes the goodness it shows to others in such settings, even when childhood taught it to doubt and defend and attack. Not surprisingly, Cayce put small-group sharing at the center of adult-growth aids. Coping goes best when others tell us—not once, but often—that we did what we could, and that the world still wants and likes us, wounded and weird as we are.

The artists and the poets among us understand that severe crisis changes us permanently. When the loss is to death or desertion or betrayal, after real intimacy and joint creation, then an empty place, a kind of tunnel to nowhere, is left right in the middle of our chests, though only the discerning may notice it. As therapists we tell our clients, for example, that when a marriage of any substance is ended, even for good reason in divorce, the loss has the weight of losing a child of the same age as the relationship. As children get older, all of us do more with them and give ourselves more fully to them, even as we receive more; so it is with a partnership. Something that had its own life is permanently lost. Not understanding this, some too readily kill a marriage in restless hunger for new conquests, as some kill a marriage in punishment for offenses borne, not realizing that inwardly each will bear the double scars of loss and murder—though the generous vines of daily preoccupations will grow over these wounds, too.

Patience, honesty, tenderness, steadfastness, gratitude—each such strand must eventually be woven into the individualized rope that is finally to guide the mind of any one of us, past the chasms of dread into the unknown that a crisis brings.

WELCOMING THE SPIRIT

The life of the spirit includes much more than prayer. It is structured by community and tradition, service and justice, study and sacrifice. But when crisis tumbles us into limbo, it is natural (as Cayce advised) to turn to prayer. At first our pleas may be nothing more than childish whimpers asking for a parent to make things all better. But pain cuts out the extraneous, and soon we may develop a serious if halting dialogue with the unseen, or just sit close to a divine Presence and forget to talk—much as we do with our dearest relatives and companions.

What tells us that we are finding our way into relationship with the divine, when we are so muddled and frightened? Gratitude does.

When we hear ourselves thanking someone for a back rub, or managing to appreciate hospital food, or mentioning that one leg still works fine, or phoning salutes to campaign workers after bitter defeat, then we are not far from the kingdom. Prayer offered in gratitude speaks of blessings not forgotten, just as the prayers of the Psalmists do, even when our hearts are broken and our minds addled.

Humility comes along with gratitude. We may ask, even scream, for divine help, and the prayer is still not awry if some part of it says, "Look, God, I haven't the foggiest idea of what to make of all this, and you'll have to take over until I do." When we admit our limitations, we free the winging spirit—so long as we do not turn it into dismal self-doubt. "Not my will but Thine be done" was one of the prayer phrases most often suggested by Cayce, in confidence that the larger will would put our lesser wills right, and turn on the drive to cope.

When terrible things happen, we can easily feel that God has abandoned us. The conviction comes all too easily if others once betrayed or neglected us, or we have betrayed or neglected others (and who has not?). Suffering and shaken, we can too easily conclude that God has chosen to punish us. The conscience keeps a ready list of failings to use for prosecuting us before the Judge, who looks much more like our own superego than like our own best impulses toward youngsters and oldsters who get into trouble. We can surrender the questions that break the mind or smash the spirit to the Presence, which will gently take them into a space that keeps and reworks them until a later time when we are not so distraught.

The assurance that the holy or unnameable is nearby and cares may grow on us almost without our noticing. Nature looks so beautiful that we can hardly speak of it, whether it offers clean snow, sprightly birds, sobbing storms, or all-beneficent sunshine. We need to recognize, by our very openness to earth's presence, that our prayers are heard.

Music and color and texture go right to the soul, as Cayce often observed. Their presence in our lives can make conflict and harmony, building and waiting, plodding and soaring all seem possible. These are not just signs of the Companion, but partake of the actual reality our prayer seeks. Yet it is loving helpers who so often bring the divine nearest, though busy nurses and solicitous friends have no idea what we secretly guess about them: that the Light which made all things has paused to incarnate a bit in them this Tuesday, right in their flesh beside us.

What we seek in prayer seems to go better when others add their prayer to our own, or when they pray for us. As freely as we ask for a drink of water or another blanket or a phone call on our behalf, we need to ask others to pray for us, regardless of the fact that they are not notable saints or mystics. God responds to *intent*, and the intercession of someone who truly loves us may break the hearts of angels. Prayer offered for us may slip its secret vibrations into our own cells and our thoughts, to melt the hardness we didn't know was there, but which held back the transforming energy we needed.

Prayer deals with real energies. We need not demand miracles. We only need hold onto whatever tells us that unpretentious prayer may engage a "More"—as William James described it—that merges with energies of our own and those trying to help us, magnifying whatever miracle of the ordinary already heals us, makes babies sprout in the seeded womb, or makes plans sprout in the deadened mind. Resonance is a key process in prayer. We know about resonance if we have ever sung when our tune went better because others joined in, or labored in a committee where small and doubtful ideas grew into big and sturdy ones, or walked in a straggling picket line that moved an immovable corporation or government office. The Spirit is frequently a gift to the people of God acting together, not reserved to private telegrams of desperation.

Often we hesitate to ask others to pray for us, because we think we are unworthy in the cosmic scheme of things. The cure Cayce often suggested is to start praying regularly for someone else, in the very hour we ask others to intercede for us. Our hearts will believe what we do, not what we endorse. We may pick a child to pray for, or the person in the next hospital bed, or—and this is easier after the period of coping has ended—the very person who hurt us. If just muttering a bit will get the prayer started, that is where we begin. Then we can branch out into the great stream of prayer that fathers and mothers all the others: thanksgiving. We can bless the nurses or the lawyers, and the takers-over or even the undertakers, who are trying to help us. We can grin at them even in tears. A little more each day, we can bless the flowers or the books or the food somebody brought, and the phone call that was both welcome and fearsome. Doing it, we find we can ask a whole congregation of people to pray for us, or even ask somebody to set up a prayer chain, where each person calls another to join in.

Having people intercede for us at the same time or times of day, as Cayce frequently suggested, seems to magnify prayer effects. So does praying together in small devotional groups or in full-sized congregations, as he heartily encouraged. The wisdom of the human family has typically matched individual prayer with activities of corporate worship, where petitions do not drown out thanksgiving and praise, and the path for the Spirit is swept clean by honest confession, as it is lighted by the lamps of disciplined reflection. So the search for prayer aid in crisis should take us early and late into events where people of serious faith gather regularly to worship—not just for private benefits, but to amplify the sense of the Presence that is promised, and that will do more than we know how to ask, though in ways not always of our choosing.

When we are just coping, the possibility of direct support from a God we think we may have offended might seem absurd. Crisis, however, can actually provoke surprising aid. Recent decades have produced extensive research on altered states of consciousness (initially studied with chemicals, but broadened to include hypnosis, meditation, guided imagery, dreams, heightened creativity, sensory invariance, or sensory deprivation). All of these have been shown to have the capacity to facilitate mystical experience—direct awareness of the divine and of dimensions in our own nature that answer to the divine. By themselves, these procedures cannot conjure anything, as early enthusiasts found to their disappointment. But such doings can often magnify potent and even life-transforming or revelatory processes, especially when the "set" purpose is high and the "setting" of caring companions in gracious surroundings is loving and lovely.

What matters for coping in crisis is that *pain* has been shown to be a potent source for just such an altering of consciousness.

This should surprise nobody who has considered the history of ascetic disciplines, or remembered servants of God bearing hardships for the needy. Worthwhile pain, borne in a caring way, has its symbols in the hardships of persecuted but faithful Jews, and the Cross of faithful Christians. There is reason to suspect that crisis brings not only shock, but its own internal medicines to heighten awareness of the ultimate. As we pray, and others join us, we may expect to discover bits of remarkable grace. Old connections to the universe we thought we had lost may hook up even in the darkest times, partly because of the very agony that the flesh knows how to turn into aid stronger than pills, by altering consciousness.

Is the time of loss and bewilderment the right season, then, for inspired decisions? Probably not. Traditions in a number of cultures, and certainly the experience of practitioners, suggest that for months or a year after a heavy blow, major decisions and fresh projects should be put off. Often Cayce advised just such caution. No new houses, new investments, new marriages, new careers, new heroic causes. The mind is just too tired to get guidance, even though it grasps that God is very near. What cannot be postponed must be undertaken, of course: bills must be paid, bodies buried, papers filed, enemies forgiven or at least no longer cursed. But the resources of a spent mind and a depleted body should not, in all mercy and good judgment, be required for bold new beginnings.

For the same reason, vows made to God in the coping stage of crisis are not often wise and fruitful. We are tempted to bargain and to promise, of course. But none of us would require pledges of undying loyalty and service before we rescued an injured dog or a lost child. We distort God if we think the divine loves us less than this when we are distraught. Too easily the vows slip into promises not to let ourselves get hurt again, and therefore not to risk, right beside our proposed bargains with the eternal. To discover solidarity with others who suffer and know not why is to gain much from crisis, indeed. We can promise ourselves not to lose this compassion. But to try cutting deals with God is to try capturing the sunrise in a cup. Later, when coping yields to other modes, sizable overhauls of our priorities and commitments will be useful.

When we are spent and rattled, it is not fruitful to press fiercely for final answers to such questions as, "Why me?" and "Why is there suffering, anyway?" Honest questions must be asked, as the Book of Job makes clear; but we need to give ourselves plenty of time to work out answers in the companionship of God, who met us at the scene of our accident. Later we will look at some of Cayce's fresh and even exciting perspectives on the meaning of suffering.

First, though, comes the willingness just to trust in the Presence. Our psychologist friend, Herbert Puryear, tells of the man who slipped over a cliff and was barely hanging onto a branch, dangling over a chasm. He cries out for help, "Is there anyone there?" A voice of assurance answers in awesome tones from the vast depths: "Let go, my son, and I will catch you." For several moments there is utter silence. Then the fearful man calls out, "Is there anyone else there?"

Trusting the divine in the moment of crisis is no cinch. Our minds race to various theories: God has overlooked us. God wants to punish us. God does what he/she can, but some events get away. God has a larger plan, into which our losses fit as caterpillar husks serve butterflies. God needs us for a project on the next plane of existence. God is testing us. God is spurring us to greater efforts for others.

Real bravery is required to recognize that just as we cannot easily understand love—the love that reaches far beyond attraction—so we are unlikely to fathom easily the other side of love that is suffering, made possible by the very caring that suffers loss. As love is not so much to be explained as lived out, so pain of loss requires its own living out, where coping is only the beginning.

The hard times of just holding on are suitable for confession. The cry of the heart to be forgiven and accepted is ever heard, in any tradition. This is not the time for a terrified recital of naughtiness. We need to speak soberly and clearly to God, now and then, when thanksgiving—not fear—spreads the prayer carpet. We must speak about that which we left undone, but ought better to have done; and that which we enacted which ought to have been left aside. Then we lay the matter on the altar, and trust. For remembered sins are like great knives. Recognized and briefly deployed in love, they may cut through huge tangles and free us from accumulated weights. But carried about and fondled, they may cut us sorely.

If the stripped-down state that pain confers leads us to pray for those we have hurt, then it is likely we may ask them for forgiveness, too, and later offer restitution. But crusades of righteousness are too much when the issue is just to stay on horseback for another day. An accepting look, an encouraging word, a bearhug, can each convey that gates of reconciliation are open for passage some other day.

It may surprise us to discover that when we are in crisis, others are angry at us for having a major problem right now. They do not usually recognize the anger at first, because it would be so embarrassing to admit. But they can be outraged that we are getting ready to leave them by dying, or that we are going bankrupt when they expected our aid, or that we stretched our marriage until it broke.

Some of their anger is fear of having to do their own coping without our help. Some is resentment that they never lived fully enough to get into the kind of trouble we now face. Some is longing for a deeper reconciling with us that now may never come. Some is their helplessness over not being able to fix the unfixable. Some is panic that what visits us may next visit them. Whatever the source, the kindnesses of those who genuinely care can be mixed with frowns and tart responses, as well as with neglect and abandonment that can easily bewilder us. When this happens, it helps to remember that everyone's life has tucked away in it elements of quiet desperation that are kept controlled until crisis upends somebody close. So our own compassion and gentleness for helpers are required. And since the demands usually are transitory, we can often surprise ourselves by delivering just what is appropriate, because we have been needing it so badly ourselves and know precisely how it feels to the hungering heart.

Finally, coping affords some hidden blessings, by creating time and space for the Spirit as we step apart from the daily round. Or it should, if we are wise enough to receive such gifts. Hospitalization can be a blessed Blue Cross retreat in our overstimulated lives. But not all crises allow such going apart under complete care and freedom from daily hassle. Sometimes we must bury a parent one day and show up at the store to sell hosiery the next. Sometimes we must give up a dream of further education, and nobody comes to our inner funeral service. Sometimes we must just stare at the drought-scorched earth and sell the farm, without taking a day off. Yet often a major crisis buys us time and allows us to collect the love that is even nearer than we had hoped. When we get that break, we can use it well and plan better ways, if we have been learning the art of growing through crisis, to which Cayce pointed.

2

How We Are Built to Grow
Through Challenge

AFTER COPING AS WE must, our next responses to crisis should be twofold. We must seek new solutions to our predicament, and we must expect to grow in stature of personhood. Even in the first weeks or months of dark distress, we may catch glimpses of these two happier outcomes. For example, something a friend tells catches our interest, and we think we might imagine a fresh creation of our own coming out of all our pain: we could try starting a business, learning yoga, or bringing together other single parents in our community. On the other hand, we may be reading a biography and momentarily surmise that our suffering could offer as much deliverance of new selfhood as dying, if we could figure out how. Perhaps we may see a certain unfrightened dignity in the eyes of a friend who has danced with cancer and walked away, perceiving a poise and richness that might one day be our own.

This chapter is about a deep human way of growth that spontaneously helps us through all sorts of grave challenges. It is about a way of unfolding and awakening that undergirds fresh solutions and larger personhood alike. It is about inner pregnancy and delivery, as a natural resource built into each of us, which is set in motion by crisis.

Literature and biography, as well as myth and fairy tale, tell over and over how an ordinary person, faced with a sorely taxing circumstance, falls into a funk. After a period of wandering and incubation and testing, the individual strides into the problem arena with resources and stature nobody guessed. Some kind of deep growth has been at work. What is it?

CAYCE'S VIEW OF DEEP GROWTH

Too often we give the credit for major gains to our conscious efforts. We assume that the new skill, the surprising contrivance, the striking amplitude of spirit, are the consequence of ardent learning and practice, enriched by fortuitous experience. Surely the emergent person, brimming with strategies and confidence, has just worked hard and thought things out. But secretly we know better. Some part of such growth is also gift or awakening under pressing demand, from the very springs of selfhood and what we lamely call the gods. It is this dimension to which Cayce's readings point.

To follow Cayce's account of deep growth, we must postulate with him the impressive influence of the unconscious on our thought and behavior. This is so considerable that we might well call it the *coconscious*—as psychologist Carl Rogers and others have suggested about the unconscious. That part nearest to consciousness, and available to it by memory, inference, and patient inspection, Cayce calls the *subconscious*—corresponding to what Carl Jung, the Swiss psychiatrist, has described as the *personal unconscious*. Here we find memories and subliminal impressions, as well as habits, defenses, and coping strategies. Here too are roles, parental images, and controls, along with automatic skills, language and logic patterns, as well as impulses from emergent values.

Farther from consciousness is another part of the psyche that often affects us more crucially. This realm Cayce calls the *superconscious*. It is usually not directly entered by consciousness except in altered states, though it can be inferred from its production of symbols, creative solutions, and primal values. This region Cayce describes as participating in universal processes, much as Jung has proposed in postulating an objective or *collective unconscious* common to humankind.

Within the superconscious realm of the psyche, Cayce's readings give primary attention to two dynamic structures: *universal patterns* and the *soul*. The patterns are governing designs or forces, which he calls "the Creative Forces," in the universe. They reach far beyond the person, yet are accessible in principle to the individual as needed. These designs, charged with energy, shape the transhuman dance of molecules and the swing of stars, just as they do the human lifespan and the glory of the great Platonic ideals: the good, the true, the beautiful, the holy. Cayce only occasionally used the term "archetype," as Jung has done, except in counsel on the artistry of suggested "life seals." But it seems clear that his intent was similar when he spoke of universal patterns at work in the superconscious, forming the groundwork for effective problem solutions and emergent selfhood alike.

Cayce suggests that the soul is structured in a way not unlike what Jung has called the *Self*. It is charged with responsibility for a person's ultimate values, and with distilling from experience and conscious reflection what is precious to the individual's development in the sight of God. Each night, according to Cayce, the soul compares in dreams—as it does in prayerful or inspired reflection—the behavior of the person with the dearest and richest of universal patterns that the soul has grasped and chosen. To be sure, dreams and visions might emerge from and reflect or advance many levels of the psyche at work. But the overall action of the soul in sleep or waking is ever for richness and integration, as it journeys toward wholeness and productive love with God.

Two Gifts: Inner Patterns and Enlarged Personhood

In Cayce's view, the ultimate key to helpful responses to crises is the spontaneous activation of particular patterns or archetypes. Over and over, for thousands of people, Cayce traced the challenge to develop fresh "attitudes and emotions" in charged clusters of meaning and energy that spring under pressure from the superconscious and work their way into consciousness. In these times, the tough person finds true tenderness, or the gentle person finds needed strength; the artist awakens to themes of justice, the reformer to the grip of beauty; the leader learns to follow and the follower discovers how to lead. The archetypes that work the change bring two gifts—precisely the gifts that crises demand.

One gift is the *inner patterns*. They leap to life as symbols in dreams, art, and rites; they appear as activities in relationships, campaigns, ESP, intellectual movements, and the rest of vital loving and hard work. Invention of fresh solutions, in this view, is only partly a matter of conscious application. It is also decisively a matter of drawing on new configurations of energy and insight from activated patterns or archetypes in the unconscious. For example, the young bride whose loving has been limited to courtship may soon awaken to mothering. This new archetypal cluster of ultimate meanings and energies brings with it a growing sense of how to proceed with all things that parent and protect and shelter others—how the hearth focuses a home, how a protest movement must be incubated to term, and even how study generates ideas. Archetypes do not in themselves confer skills, formulate systems, teach languages, or make decisions. But they offer the crystalline shoots, the sudden sproutings of connections, the designs of tensions and proportions and stages that makes the hard work of conscious gains possible.

The other gift of the archetype, as a birthright of the soul stirred to life by challenge, is *enlarged personhood*, the transformation of self promised by crisis. For example, the student who not only memorizes and manipulates the pieces of language and mathematics and science, but through the arduous sweat of exams and study manages to fall in love with truth and finds its disciplined pursuit compelling, is not the same person as the one who first attended classes as a perfunctory ritual. Right beside this student may be another, who bears well a broken heart in a generous love affair and who may find such archetypal richness of caring as never again to be just a needy seeker of intimacy.

For Cayce, the twin process of using freshly activated patterns of "forces" for useful creations and enlarged individuality is the essential business of karma, whether conducted in one lifetime or many. (Cayce's view of karma is discussed in detail in chapter six.) One of the great adventures of exploring the inner world, from his perspective, is learning how such a process works in one's own life, by tracking specific growth episodes that follow on such heavy challenges as crises. Cayce insisted over and over to those who sought his aid, "Study self and self's experiences." Thoughtful and patient attention to the inner drama can teach the nature of deep growth, minimize detours and traps, and maximize helpful resources.

FOUR AIDS TO STUDYING DEEP GROWTH

If we are to make sense out of the diversity in crisis-born growth—which means making sense out of being a live adult—we will profit by four primary aids: keeping a journal; reading biographies, novels, and myths; sharing with companions; and—when possible—exploring our dreams. The subject of dreams is so large that we will discuss it separately.

Keep a Journal

Keeping a journal, or a running oral dialogue with a few close companions, or both, allows us to make records and analyze trends and processes in our lives, across months or even years. Many people use a journal to track their dreams. Others use it more to converse with their inner selves and with God, as they note daily experiences and inward responses. Sooner or later, most people who keep journals use them to make drawings, develop lists and self-inventories, or undertake planned experiments. For we are not here taking a course in cooking or sailing, or acquiring some goodies for conversation. We are working on the grown-up art of growth itself.

Into the journal can go indicators of the stirrings of growth or pregnancy in the unconscious. These may be as innocuous as slips of the tongue, or as awesome as gripping moods. In time, there will likely be pages for memories, sorted thematically for their treasures and trash about vocation, mating, personhood, and more. Spiritual stirrings and intuitions belong in such journals—about nature, meditation, worship, or just the absorbed faces of rope-skipping children. Above all, we seek illuminating connections that may reveal archetypal patterns in our doings, such as people who have won our deep interest, and when and with what consequences. As cave men and women once drew bears and bison and birds on the walls, so we must draw designs—in words or symbols or both—that reflect the ways in which we are shattered or shaken and then made whole and richer by our challenges.

Reading Biographies, Fiction, and Myth

Self-inspection without interpretive materials may run dry for any but poets and prophets. So along with a personal journal we need a flow of growth episodes from the lives of other people of some amplitude. Biographies are treasures for the wondering adult. We can learn equally from the sternly disciplined Gandhi or the impassioned Martin Luther, the crusading Sigmund Freud or the tormented Vincent Van Gogh. The scriptures of the great religions carry their many burdens on the backs of biographies. The histories of these traditions offer further treasures of life accounts, long after the founders have become legends: Ramakrishna of India, worshiping black Mother Kali; the Baal Shem Tov of Polish Judaism, dancing and teaching and healing; Francis of Assisi, starting naked into his new life after his youth as a playboy.

Novels, plays, and films that grapple with growth episodes in their successive stages and possible outcomes can also be useful. Captain Ahab in *Moby Dick* illuminates the search for the white whale of the Other that lives in all of us, with its potential for both grandeur and destruction. The plays of Eugene O'Neill and William Shakespeare depict a variety of human crises. The death of Willy Loman, who tried clumsily to take on needed growth, has a certain fierce nobility, as we see in Miller's *Death of a Salesman*; but death from avoiding the sting of such a challenge makes Shakespeare's *Hamlet* everyone's guide to the inner world. Similarly, the archetype of tender compassion both ennobles and destroys the earnest ruler in *The King and I*.

Fairy tales and myths offer their own telling insight into the way change comes about within us. Beauty, who serves the Beast out of love for her father, grows into her own womanly love of the unlovable, which transforms her companion into a human. Psyche, in the myth of Amor and Psyche, takes on the challenges of womanhood, one by one; Parsifal does the same for manhood. Both discover they can only be themselves when they incarnate something of the other gender, too.

Sharing with Companions

The third aid to exploring serious growth is *sharing* with like-minded companions. An expensive, though life-transforming method may be psychotherapy—especially if done with a guide who knows literature and mythology, religions and comic strips. Spiritual directors or seasoned companions are available nowadays in a number of religious communities, at little or no financial cost (but of course embodying other demands that give new meaning to the old cry: "Your money or your life!"). Yet we can often derive the same benefit from friends in a sharing group that incarnates honest relatedness. Groups must avoid such aborting of community as M. Scott Peck describes in *The Distant Drum*: pretending oneness, and trying hastily to fix and instruct each other, instead of being vulnerable to one another and receiving the gifts of mutual, pain-won insight. Religious communities and spiritual groups are often so focused on dramatic change that they fasten tenaciously onto a few classic scripture tales or normative teachings on how-to-make-it, born again. But the best do it in dialogue with contemporary existence, where the call of Moses is set beside the transfer of today's business executive, and the crises of Job are anyone's loss of children and spouse in a divorce. Christopher Fry understood that the helpful Bible stories are those laid bare beside tonight's dreams, where we are all somehow prisoners backing into glory that we thought would incinerate us.

THE SPECIAL AID OF DREAMS

Our dreams, which we so often allow to slip out of reach in the night, can be bright candles to lead us through crises to inventiveness and growth. Cayce began systematically to interpret dreams for seekers in 1923, when they were still used chiefly by psychiatrists for the mentally ill. He helped dozens of individuals use these aids to the inner world for two decades, in hundreds and hundreds of readings for that purpose. Repeatedly he showed how dreams helpfully mirror *all* our daily concerns for creative outcomes.

Not all of us are equally served by dream study. The young need to handle dreams with care, lest the inner world become more fascinating than the real world. So do those who have not yet put down the great anchors for the ships of their lives: loving and working. But grown-ups who want to grow even further up may find in dreams and associated reveries (including inspired altered states) much more than the trolls and dragons of repressed sex and violence.

As modern laboratories have captured and unpacked for study the busy dreams of thousands of ordinary subjects, they have shown the psyche judiciously tracking and neatly symbolizing the progress of growth episodes themselves. Indeed, they have shown dreams advancing the action, not just mirroring it. Just as we engage in rites by day—whether of marrying or burying, bossing or electing—so we take on powerful values and forces in those individualized rites of the night, which dreams essentially are; in dreams, we move life energy through its appointed rounds to fresh growth. Accordingly, when we work with dreams, we do not decode strange symbols. Rather, we befriend dream contents, until the nighttime work of rebalancing the psyche and reworking its dynamics is met by daytime activities and relationships that enhance the spells and competence we need. Setting out to use the special resource of dreams is not embarking on a journey to be smart about hidden matters. It is trying to be whole and potent, under the blessing of remembered and rehearsed dreams.

Recalling Our Dreams

The art of recalling weighty dreams needs practice, like any other worthwhile skill. In the university psychology classes we have personally taught, it has been an adventure to show students that virtually all can recall dreams if they choose to do so. Crisis-wounded adults are a bit more complicated than students, but we also have

shown thousands of these how to do dream recall. The first requirement is a real interest in the inner world, and that usually means
having one or more friends or relatives, or a group, in which to share
some dreams and other inner material fairly regularly; it also means
reading books and articles on dreaming, and on growing whole yet
risking much.

The next requirement for recall is to practice selective vigilance.
Anyone who can set the mind to waken for catching a plane or keeping an appointment can set it to waken to write down or remember
hefty dreams. Since dreams occur in a stage just below waking, after
deeper sleep, it is no great trick to go the extra distance to full arousal,
briefly, while we rehearse a dream or write down enough of it to
shove it from short-term into long-term memory.

We must take care not to lose dreams. Moving the body before
retrieving dreams often jars the fragile recall out of reach, as Cayce
pointed out decades before sleep laboratories tracked this phenomenon. Not getting enough sleep keeps us from embarking on the last
and usually longest dream of the night, or indeed from wanting any
arousal at all during our sleep. Alcohol and certain other drugs, including some commonly used for heart patients, may impair recall or
drastically affect dream content. We may also confront an ethical
challenge to dream recall, when we have been through a frightening
crisis or change in our lives and have consciously or unconsciously
resolved not to think or even dream about the painful episode. Although the unconscious goes on reworking and regrouping our experiences and relationships all our lives, toward deeper insight and
growth, it does not give up recall of its dream treasures to those who
say to it, "Yes, but." We must tell ourselves that nothing is off limits,
and to trust that the unconscious will deal with us gently in the
night—as it usually does until we can take stronger food and drink
from its table.

Interpreting Our Dreams

Interpretation begins from the moment we rehearse in mind or write
down a dream. Making notes at bedside is often best for beginners.
Even as we choose phrases and images (best written in the present

tense) to tell ourselves what transpired and where, and how the characters felt, we can feel little tugs of extra meaning or weight. Underlining these words or phrases that pop out at us can be helpful in separating the central from the incidental in the dream content, and can start us down the merry road of interpreting.

Studying and making friends of one's dreams is a matter of correlating them with waking life. The first task is to list and mull over what is happening in large areas of one's life: love and relationships, work and study, growth and faith, and selfhood in its physical, mental, and spiritual dimensions. We can then sort our dreams into piles that seem to match these concerns. When we dream centrally of working in a shop or office or a particular field, the drama deserves immediate consideration for its possible relevance to our everyday labors—although further reflection may assign it somewhere else, but only for compelling reasons.

Once we get a slippery dream into the right general nets of reference, we need to strip it down to a skeletal statement of content: for example, "Two women go to market, where one loses a purse and the other lags behind out of fear of ruffians." Simple as these generic synopses are, we can find in the bare summaries resonance with what is troubling or challenging a particular part of our lives, such as employment that threatens identity (purse) and too often belittles (ruffians). Then we can see where the action is headed, before we return to interpret the full nocturnal play.

Actually, we all know thousands of quite conscious plots and their import already, so that matching dreams with them for hints of interpretation is not as difficult as it might seem. We have a native repertoire from nursery rhymes and ditties, TV and films and books and plays, and untold songs and comic strips and even commercials, as well as the little dramas implicit in familiar speech images, such as, "He fell for her." Equipped with such bountiful comparative resources, and reminded that it is we ourselves who concocted the dream for reasons some part of us already knows, we can venture boldly into interpretation. We can feel secure that a dream or series of dreams—and a series is the better focus for skilled interpretation—will likely repeat if wrongly handled.

Cayce made it a point to start most of his dream interpretations in trance readings by assigning particular dreams to regions of the psyche that do markedly differing kinds of business with consciousness. Jung did the same in principle by relating them to the personal or impersonal layers of the unconscious. Neither offered a method much conducive to using a dream dictionary, except for helpful practice. Such lists of symbols tend to blur distinctions between weighty or archetypal images and those drawn from daily bustle. But making a lexicon of symbols in one's own dreams, informed by reading or talking with others who work regularly with dreams, is not only helpful, but probably essential to systematic dream use.

Like any other art, we will master the principles and practical strategies of interpreting dreams only by trying again and again. Interpreting dreams by some clever act of decoding is not nearly as important as trying sensitive responses to them. Sharing them, drawing them, taking up a new course of action suggested by them, trying a fresh tack with self-study and self-training—all of these receive the gifts of dreams into the living flows of the busy psyche. There is much to suggest that dreams function more to sensitize and motivate us than to give us messages. The true dream impact is found in the next day's choices well-made.

Seasoned dream catchers report that working patiently with dreams has much the same effect as working with one's own poetry. The products become clearer, more pointed, more eloquent. So growing with one's dreams is not just remembering them nor cracking them, but keeping up a dialogue with them, until they tend toward terse haiku. Generalizing on what we learn in dreams—to help us handle the symbolisms in our illnesses, our compulsions, our clothing choices and movie preferences, as well as how we relate to our companions—also works to clarify the flow. All the enacting and dramatizing and spinning of spells in our lives streams from the same sources within us, and draws on the same themes-in-progress.

THE EIGHT STAGES OF THE DEEP GROWTH PROCESS

Carl Jung gave the rather inelegant name of "complex" to the familiar human experience of becoming a different person with new resources as a result of encountering challenges that shake us. He was looking for a neutral word that might suffice, whether the outcome were gain or breakdown. To him, the process was potentially healthful and normal for everyone, meant to produce new life as a kind of conception and gestation leading to the birth of new personhood. Popular psychology has reserved the term complex for crippling hang-ups, as in the familiar labels of "mother complex," "authority complex," "inferiority complex," or "Messiah complex." But Jung had in view a growth sequence so basic to human existence that he sometimes called his entire psychological system "Complex Psychology," rather than its better-known name of "Analytical Psychology." He was pointing to episodes of deep growth, with archetypal foundations, such as engaged Cayce's attention.

Like Jung, Cayce emphasized that the gifts of archetypes may be fully claimed only by those well grounded in consciousness who are willing to risk. Distress may precipitate growth episodes or complexes of inner pregnancy. But they can only proceed to term and yield their treasures for a disciplined consciousness that is ready to handle them. Some may seek shortcuts by plundering the unconscious in altered states, but the gift of archetypes is reserved for those willing to spend much. The prodigal son of Jesus' parable may have found a bountiful father, ready to embrace and feed and celebrate him. But the son's way led through indulgence and even pigpens, until he saw some truths and made some humbling choices. The elder brother, who stayed home, got love from the same father, but showed neither the wits nor the large-hearted stature that come from picking up one's inheritance and putting it somewhere, for worse or better—or both.

It takes patience to track the growth process through its stages and discovering what helps or hinders its work. Most of us are working on several themes at once, some major and some minor. Further, there is no fixed pregnancy term (although most of us have a kind of personal gestation cycle that gets us into something new and important every few years or so). At any given time, one archetype may be well along toward delivery of its precious gifts, while another may be tardy—we only know that something keeps creating the same frustrating predicaments. Finally, our psychological pregnancies, unlike those of the flesh, can continue all the way to delivery and yet spiral over the same themes in further growth episodes, more richly each time. But what seasoned parent thinks that birthing a child is the last delivery of that offspring?

We can trace eight stages, any of which may be telescoped into its neighbors, in the lifespan of a growth episode that yields a new universal pattern or archetype, such as Cayce described. Learning to recognize these stages in our behaviors and feelings, as well as in our dreams, and to harvest their fruits for problem solving and enriched personhood is a giant step into the art of growing through personal crisis.

Stage 1: Call to Deep Growth

What creates a growth episode? Typically, it is an inner demand to produce better, to love more generously, to stand fast, or to evince some other human capacity that seems beyond our reach. Some challenges merely require us to work harder, get specialized aid, or accept reasonable limitations. But other challenges are more difficult: the load of single parenting falls on us, and we must somehow be both father and mother to the brood; sudden job loss requires that we take up a new calling; the impairment of an organ or a limb curtails our activities outrageously. Then the unconscious, like the keeper of a far kingdom, begins to organize its powerful expeditions to help us.

Some difficult challenges arrive slowly. For example, we finally step into the long-destined leadership of a family firm; an ailing parent finally dies; our mistakes at work finally catch up with us. Sooner or later, the strategies and armor we each carry as adults will encounter a worthwhile battle where they simply won't prevail. Alfred Adler, the Viennese psychiatrist and colleague of Freud and Jung, spoke of two kinds of inferiority complexes in everyone's life. The first appears in childhood, where adults seem powerful and arbitrary, until life confers on us adolescent fury and fantasy, followed by adult independence. But then comes the second devastating discovery: in some major adult task we simply must take on, we see to our horror that we really *are* inferior. At that point the stage of the call to new stature and competence begins.

To be sure, the real call or mysterious beckoning from destiny must have a secret resonance within us, when we or those close to us murmur, "You can, if you must." Merely announcing goals of ambition or tranquility does not constitute a call from the gods, and coveting the lot of others breaks a great commandment. The call presents itself as something we cannot refuse, without forsaking our souls. In Jung's view of the complex, as in Cayce's view of the growth episode and karma, the resources of all recurrent human experience are in principle available to us. Utter dismay and pain split open our inner earth and show us a path to depths we did not guess were there.

While the call is at work, we see evidence of our circumstances everywhere, like it or not. The world is suddenly full of children of divorced parents, or reassigned executives, or cancer patients, or students forced to drop out of school. We find all around us people remarkably like us: leaders divided against themselves, lovers who must stand in love when they would rather fall there, elders who must give away their icons just to fit into a retirement apartment. Guilt assails us, suggesting that there is more we should be doing, even when we are totally unsure of what it is. Fantasies dance into the mind, with images of trips abroad, delicious seductions, sudden fame, or telling the boss off at last. We resolve to try harder, and make ferocious efforts to keep busy, or to cope with impressive speed. Often the redoubled investment works for a time, and the call is muted. But if it is a genuine beckoning from both outer happening and inner selfhood, it returns. Frequently we do not even know what is being asked of us, only that we are bugged and bothered and restless. Something momentous is afoot, but what? The call brings a signal to pay attention, but rarely proclaims its full intent.

Dreams signal a call to new becoming with plots of intruders, ringing phones, being called by name, knocks on the door or on the head, baffling mechanical malfunctions, letters or bills, and messengers who may be cosmic, archaic, or mundane carrying portent with their parcels. Sometimes the call comes with a shaft of unearthly light, or soaring music (such as the shepherds heard at Bethlehem), or sudden stillness in the midst of activity. One way or another the dream proclaims with Linda, the wife of Willy Loman in *Death of a Salesman*, "Attention must be paid. A man is dying." But the death announced is not the death of the body, but the death of our old selves, to make ready for the new.

We must now be patient and pay attention. We would like to read another wise book, attend another inspiring lecture, or otherwise suddenly improve our lot; but the part of us that is soul does its thing, all in its own time, and usually not what we would devise if asked. Nature may help us remember that growth goes in seasons, or prayer and meditation and worship may link us to the Unhurried. If we want the help that is appointed for us, we must wait upon it with as much grace as we can muster, not forgetting to give thanks for past rivers we crossed or private Berlin walls we scaled, in our personal sagas.

Stage 2: Blocking

Stage 2, blocking, is similar to denial. In this period, we try to over-power the problem or run away. Something in us freezes, and does not want the responsibility of new life—not right now. We blame or attack others, for a problem that has begun to crack our wits and disrupt our sleep as we enlist sympathizers and fellow blamers. This time of evasion is not petty; it is necessary to let resources gather deep within us. While we are protesting, or taking a trip, or resolutely cleaning the garage, or even having an affair, the developing arche-type is gathering its own energies, well hidden from consciousness. We seek out the comfortable and familiar, eat steaks or seafood, tele-phone friends, and persist in affirming, "Not me! I'm not ready."

If further education is part of the call, we disparage mere degrees and credentials. If unwanted parenting is proposed, we explain that our days are already too crowded by important assignments. If it is time to do business with a real God, we spout astrology or ESP in knowing tones. But our emotions are surprisingly close to the sur-face, and not the confident moods we want. Besides, we get unac-countably tired, as though something in us were headed for incuba-tion, and we sleep in fetal position or take warm, womb-like baths, telling ourselves we are just fighting off a virus that is going around.

Dreams in the blocking period present motifs that can be ex-tended for months or longer if we flout destiny with our wills. They often present us with problems of twos: two cars, two babies, two bridges, two roads—any doubleness that suggests our divided wills. Or they feature barriers such as we have inwardly contrived, whether fences or walls, costumed disguises or pretenses. Not uncommonly, dreams of blocking include stopped-up toilets or sinks, or garbage that needs to turn into compost instead of rotting stink, or elevators that go nowhere we want to reach. In our dreams we are late to class, late to meetings, late for lovemaking; we can't remember where we parked our car, where we put our wallet, or even where we left the baby. We are not prepared to speak in public, play a role in a drama, deliver a business report, or be tested in school. We find ourselves naked in public places, or see—when our defenses have taken over—that we are surrounded by snow and ice that signify all-covering smooth repression.

Now we must decide to yield our wills to a larger Will; to step by choice, not desperation, into the flow of happenings that has arisen within us. If we do not, the body itself will eventually assure us a retreat, by an illness or accident, or a calamity of affairs that requires us to rely on others, reminding us that life is compounded of both effort and release. Running away and hiding is a common human evil, easily forgiven when we stop it. What gives us real trouble is contriving a fake existence and demanding that others now accept it. When we tell ourselves in bravado that we never really wanted the lost lover, did not expect our new consulting firm to make it, or suspected God would test us by taking the baby away, we may remove ourselves to safety for a time, but shut the doors and windows to the Spirit that can make all things fresh and different. A choice that will recur now makes its appearance: to take a direction, for better or worse, but to allow it to be corrected as we go. The ship whose rudder is lashed down does very poorly among rocks.

Stage 3: Downswing

The next stage seems to be a movement downward, but it is really inward. Vital energy begins to flood to the roots of our beings, to engage and support new life there. Consequently, the energy may not be available where we want it for daily activity. We are tired, bushed, spent, even though we sleep or laze around. We alternate between compulsive activity and not caring much for anything. Associates tell us to take a break, go to a movie, go to Hawaii, go shopping—or go to hell! Often these admonitions help, and a sheer change of setting and activity may start us thinking and feeling that change is in the air, as it certainly is for us. But as inner energy slips farther out of reach, we begin to grasp that distraction won't cut it, and start making lists of what might really be the problem. We stare at our dream records, and draw comfort from loving letters or phone calls. Still the tumble continues.

During this period, we may often experience heightened sexuality. The vital energy has gone inside to first things, to the generative powers. Everyone—strangers, people in commercials, those in worship—suddenly looks delicious. These randy currents, more fitting for runaway adolescence, are actually signs of the life force itself—determined to reduce us to essentials and keep us going. Soldiers waiting out a siege, mourners just back from funerals, students who have lost scholarships, athletes suddenly past their prime, retired people who have golfed or goofed off enough, the painfully divorced—all report flashing visits from the angel of eroticism, painting every scene in flesh tones. Not surprisingly, we may try to calm the primal storms by seduction, and find some solace and even hints of the rebalancing yin and yang that may be afoot. But copulation by itself won't substitute for inner conception and lasting growth, though it may help with its ancient dance of opposites reconciled.

As the burgeoning growth episode robs us of energy, we are irritated by items we have misplaced, or by pushy creditors. We have waves of fear and even downright panic at times, wondering if we will ever be ourselves again. We eat more, but often enjoy it less. We even ask whether this is what getting ready to die is like. And almost always we get sick. The body itself suffers; its resistance is down. Sniffles or coughs are strangely like weeping, and upsets of digestion or defecating seem peculiarly fitting for what we can't swallow or bear as excrement in our lives. Old aches and organ weaknesses return, like marauding foxes raiding the chickens when they see fences down, or muggers on streets where we walk with too-hesitant steps. Tears, or the longing for them, may plague us, when the TV show touches us unaccountably, or the sunny child bouncing a ball reminds us of our own lost innocence.

As might be expected, dreams of the downswing are graphic. We drive a car that rolls backwards, or get into an elevator that fails to stop, or walk into quicksand. The terrain is puddled and muddy, we are nearly suffocated, someone is held hostage, we strike at enemies who feel nothing. A pet gets sick, a boat sinks, robbers make off with our stereo and television equipment. Whatever can signify loss and depletion without scaring us to death pops up in nightly dramas. That here and there we see light at the end of a tunnel, or a baby alive and crying in a deserted warehouse, or flowers growing on a dangerous battlefield, should tell us that the deep inner growth knows where it is going. But since we do not yet know consciously, the comfort is brief. Rain and storms are common, equal to our tears, and uncanny winds make them worse. Creatures stalk us, and life seems reduced to survival. We lie awake, wondering what is happening to us.

In the downswing we need a gift of courage from consciousness. Just as a pregnant woman worries that her fetus might not have the right limbs and organs, but knows that the shaping is beyond her, so the person invested with pregnancy of selfhood must give room to forces that can be trusted to do their formative, enlivening work. Knowing the lore of those who have been there and made it helps. Christians may feel powerful constructive rhythms below the surfaces of their lives during Lent and Easter, just as Muslims during Ramadan sense that from what is released in fasting for a month, much else may be gained. Raw courage is not easily stockpiled, and sometimes the first step to free the downswing begins with a literal stride: a trip, a hike, a voyage. Any pattern that says pilgrimage is helpful to the sequences that must here prevail. Rites of comfort and embrace are also useful. Whoever cradles and strokes a pet or a child in this time also gently rocks the unseen inner help that is gathering its unique strength and character for the tasks yet to confront consciousnesss.

Stage 4: Waiting

Grown men and women who have been through the waiting period shudder to remember it. Unlike pregnancy, which is over in nine months, inner growth takes all the time it requires. To be sure, most of us have been through it several times, without naming the process, by the age of maturity. We have sweated out starting school, facing bullies, being left out by cliques, being intoxicated by a gorgeous or handsome teacher, climbing the dizzying tree of orgasm, having to move to another city. We have been ill or injured, and faced the death of someone essential to our lives. So waiting for something new to come to life, when we are growing a new selfhood and new resources, is not unthinkable, though it often seems unbearable. When the challenge is not simply to adjust, or to grow up, but to grow around a permanent loss that changes us forever, the waiting may seem cruel. Fortunately, the body cooperates. It wants to rest, to go inward. If we won't let it, then it visits us with infections, or devises interruptions that slow us down anyway.

We think we can't do anything right during the waiting period, and often do not want to try. Failures are typical of this time, because our vital energy is being used for better things; but they only seem to prove our inadequacy. We feel helpless, and doubt our identity and worth. When we try to haul up our massive problem, known or unknown, to inspect it afresh, we encounter the seaweed effect—as when a raised anchor brings up everything from the ocean floor. A lost lover reminds us of all other lost loves, and of desolate times in childhood. A lost opportunity for advancement brings with it letters we neglected to write, or classes we failed, or poor career choices. When friends offer to talk things over with us, we think it is really not worth their time, and make up excuses to get out of the embarrassing exchanges, which could only issue in their seeing behind our masks what we think in fact lives there: too little, too late.

The experiences and feelings in the waiting time are so close to clinical depression, because they are genuine despair and doubt, that many conclude they are mentally ill. They sometimes get certified and medicated, when they are not sick at all, only pregnant. Any expectant mother in the last waiting weeks can testify to boundless fatigue and ennui, even when raptures of planned cuddling are not far away. Just so, sleep, rest, and food beckon in the waiting stage. The expectant psyche has to give of its primal resources to something that is reworking all systems for new values and behaviors, not just new skills. If the deep psyche, under the guidance of what Cayce called the soul, is about to give us willpower, or concern for the underdog, or visions of glory with God to command the rest of our days, it takes its sweet time, making sure that the gift will be implanted in all our flesh and thinking. We distinguish episodic depletion from real depression by self-examination. Can we locate the low feelings in a framework that has a beginning, a middle, and a possible end, as a growth cycle? Or are we experiencing a bitter self-rage, or an unmourned grief?

Dreams in the waiting time show us flooded basements and neighborhoods, wilted plants, stagnant sinks and drains, a labyrinth, or a road with too many forks. We find we cannot awaken in the dream, or that our feet will not move when we try to run, or that when we seek to swim to the surface we can't find which way is up. We are scared by funerals and corpses, although the experience of skilled dream interpreters suggests that we are seeing the death of old patterns and limited values in ourselves, preparatory to new life, rather than our own demise (which is more often pictured as a great voyage, a tribal rite, or that noble attainment, by the deep unconscious that knows things about survival of death are hidden from consciousness). When very large changes within us are afoot, symbolism becomes cosmic. We are the last ones alive after a bomb, or visited by a space ship, or confronted by a dragon. Or we may be tugging at a sword in a stone, or kneeling before the throne of God. Indeed, the presence of clearly mythic or cosmic material signals that the waiting will soon be over, for inner vital energy has found the roots of the hills and set up its camp with the eternal.

During the waiting period we must yield up our helplessness and offer the best we have. We may not simply bargain for relief; for what we see as Satan's mindless torment can actually be a messenger from God, if we follow Job's analysis. But a great emptying of pettiness and pushiness is fitting. In this way, we can bring simple flowers to the grave of our unworthy or childish elements, which might block new growth.

We may make promises. Dream scenes of a coming wedding or caring for a new baby, each requiring solemn commitments, may echo into waking appreciation of similar events, just as we may find ourselves kneeling and offering prayer in both the dream and the waking aftermath.

Stage 5: False Starts

As the waiting comes to the close of its term, energy begins to arrive along with new interests and appetites. We long to do something decisive to get out of the Slough of Despond and stay out. So we make heroic lunges—trying whatever has worked in the past, or following the advice of friends—to experience the temporary relief that comes with at least *doing* something. False labor pains are a useful analogy, except that in dealing with the growth episode or complex we may leap on a knife and try to do our own cesarean.

This is the time, as a wise observer has noted, when we make long distance calls, usually several. We can find enough energy to talk, and enough hope to suspect that there is an answer somewhere to what has been dragging us along. Or we may write letters to cherished friends and relatives, detailing our pilgrimage of recent months. We may sit down and bravely plan for a new job, a new kind of marriage, a new devotional life, or new physical fitness. We may well do a deep self-inventory, with or without professional aid. Each effort brings a hint of promise, a whiff of spring to our wintry landscape. But often we are tempted to move from outer formulas, rather than inner promptings. We copy someone else's solution, mimic someone else's confidence, talk to someone else's God. All too often we will encounter devotees of various solutions, who are ready to show us that we need baptizing in their waters. They say, if only we would read the works of Yogananda or Gurdjieff, or Jung or Cayce, or Teilhard de Chardin or Eckhart, we would see the Big Picture and know what we have been lacking. If only we would claim our true feminism, our true sexuality, our true rage, our true pacifism, our true relation to Mother Earth, our true need of salvation, our true vulnerability to complexes, we would have the key to this and future troubles.

But joining solemn or noisy assemblies may be a regrettable trap during this stage. By becoming devotees, or even jumping into a job with a promising firm or a coupling with a wounded soulmate, we may trap ourselves in the very trough we need to climb out of. In an age when media and mailings offer all sorts of menus, and people who could be tribal elders are too often left behind where we grew up, the means for discriminating false starts from true beginnings can be sparse.

Dreams can help. A dance that swirls nowhere is a warning even while it invites us to get moving. A beached ship, a junked car, a hobbled horse, all suggest travels that are not quite right. A bridge may be promising, but not if it leads to a dead end. The garden that is more weeds than blossoms, the pet that limps, the child that cries from neglect, all tell us that new life is possible, but not without discrimination. Food that feeds others but runs out for us, ordinary bills that arrive with outrageous totals, circles of community that collapse on themselves—these are invitations not to be hasty, but to stay the course.

The journal, if it has been well used, can rescue us from many false starts or too-wide detours. Our journal should contain (as Cayce never wearied of suggesting) formulations of our deepest ideals, and citations of our own personal saints—those individuals of manifest integrity and lovely spirits who often appear in dreams, and whom Cayce called "criterion figures."

Our personal experience has shown us that everyone builds up touchstones of reality, everyone devises a medicine pouch of worthwhile memories, whether we aim at these or not. In the time of the hasty heart, when false starts beckon because they are so nearly correct, we need to hunker down and consult our beads, our compasses, our icons. Then we wait a little longer, and find ourselves grateful for the lures, because they helped us get clearer about the real change and growth appointed to us.

Stage 6: Turning

When the time of turning is at hand, others see it in us before we find it in ourselves. They note the resurrected smiles, watch the gait get jaunty, catch bursts of deep conviction, hear the hush of proportion forming in our appreciations. Much of what is about to happen is gift, as the psyche brings forth the rich complex it has nurtured so patiently, and presents its archetypal wisdom and energy to consciousness for disposal.

A turning is required—not simply a ripening. Now the role of consciousness, of will and insight and choice, is crucial. We have to come down somewhere, take a direction, bet on an understanding, trust a relationship—or all of these at once. A complex (which may well be a manifestation of karma, as Cayce suggested) can hang around the back door for weeks or even months, while we sit in the living room and wait for it to announce itself. But we must go to the door, look it in the eye, and welcome it—even if the cost is dispatching a phony dream, ending a shabby relationship, or taking the risk of bankruptcy on principle. We must act in wide-awake whole-souled choice, not under any spell. Nobody else can tell us, finally, what we must do.

The turning that is right for us is ever *to the light,* not just away from darkness. Trying to *avoid* sin and evil, pain and regret, won't do it. When we make our move it must be with sunshine in view, for ourselves and others—especially for others. When Willy Loman kills himself to give his son a fresh start with the insurance money, we understand that he made his best play, given his values, even though the solution was crazy and not free from guilt or self-pity. The hint that he was turning to the light came when he tried to plant some seeds in his garden, living out an old dream impossible where nothing but sidewalk remains. It is ever the presence of living things, sprouting, playing, blooming, brawling, that signals which way to turn when the moment of truth is at hand. It is possible to sacrifice, even to die, when the turning is toward happy faces given freedom, not to judges who are never big enough to understand.

Our dreams facilitate the turning, although they are powerless to make it for us. They feature children, full of innocence and play; couples tenderly fondling each other; fair winds blowing. They offer new clothing, fresh colors, the calm after a storm, simple food to share, and remarkable solutions to impossible mechanical, electrical, or plumbing problems. They show us that we can climb up on the dead bones of the past, or swim toward a patch of clear light, or claim an award. They draw a mandala where round and square meet and all sides are heard from, or deal in great old rocks and sturdy trees. We are in motion in such dreams, making choices or apportioning tasks or singing songs. For this is the day which consciousness must make, though it prepares the way for the Lord of the Dance.

For better or for worse, for richer or poorer, to prevail in sickness and in health, we draw from the growth episode its gift of shining force, containing truth and energy, as well as values and forthcoming relationships. When this step is rightly made—without asking for shortcuts or miracles, but only to be more fully alive and awake after the sleep of our incubating prison—the consequences are striking.

Stage 7: Upswing

The upswing period has the feel of miracles. Fully workable ideas suddenly come tumbling into mind. We can design an entire house, or map out a campaign, or figure out what to say to an alienated teenager. We can make some sense of the universe, and discriminate a spiritual teaching from a mere spiritual pitch. We want to clean house, catch up on letters, plant the garden, buy new equipment, go see friends. A trip would be inviting, but just tearing into a sunny or comfortably drizzly day is often trip enough. Purged by pain and humbled by waiting, we can be truly elated, if we are genuinely thankful. Energy pours through the flesh, and a brisk walk feels like a parade march before the gods. Pets are for happy teasing, babies are for diapering, children are for swinging, and even stubborn colleagues are there to make us grow while we help them in turn. These are not shallow responses, but heartfelt.

When tests come, we find that something strong and sure has

grown in us. We can meet the suspicious and touchy ex-spouse without having to hurt anyone, because we're headed into new life. We can hug a husband or lover who seemed too little involved in an abortion, because the missing life force grows in him, too. We can pick up a wrecked career and find that some of the pieces fit into a new design that never seemed possible before. One or more freshly available archetypes are at work, in no uncertain fashion, bringing solutions and bringing personhood.

Dreams move smartly along with the upswing, giving it steady force and balance. Elevators run where we tell them, cars can be steered, flowers grow by the road, beautifully crafted jewelry appears, rivers flow freely, planes take off, and the water bobs us along as we swim. Peasants dance, animals gallop in a free-ranging herd, and we move into a new house or office with companions who are tender, wise, and determined.

The joy of the upswing can be so rich that we are tempted to ride it forever, like a stallion that never has to be fed or harnessed. But interpenetration of consciousness is the watchword of real growth, and conscious consolidation comes next. Another complex is surely already forming somewhere in our depths, waiting for the jolt of outer demand to set it loose on its course, like a comet in our inner space. Or the same archetypal growth motif, which we now know can confer on us peership in the best of adult life, consults its royal scrolls and prepares to send us another cryptic demand to stretch.

Stage 8: Integration

While the gift of the gods is still with us, we have work to do. First comes thanksgiving, best done before cherished others, though also done in the stillness of earnest devotion to the Ultimate. Gifts claimed without hearty gratitude seem too much like private attainments, won by heroic enduring. We have a fatted calf to cook and a party to throw, not once but a number of times, remembering to invite the elder brother of the parable who has yet to make his move and trouble the deeps where archetypes and universal patterns lie. Ritual appreciation won't cut it, but taking a youngster to the zoo might, and planning a career with space for the underdog is the kind of gratitude that means business.

We need to establish guidelines; we may write them out in a journal, or tell them to friends. We have a grace period, while we are saying grace over our growth, in which we can think clearly and deeply about what matters most in our lives. Now is the time, not in haste but in deliberate action, to decide whether and how we ought to get rich or famous, or get learned or adored. Life goals can be overhauled with lasting effect, in the integration period, and we can lay a keel for the ship of our selfhood that will take us to far and lovely places, though not without pain and shipwrecks. And now is the time to make promises to the One—not for favors, but for the delight of it. It is the time to write a letter for forgiveness, and to pay back old thefts of time or patience, of love or belongings.

The wisdom of the human family reminds us to use this period so that we can meet the next blow with more trust and a better sense of timing. We can afford to look back, ask what made things go better or worse, and then arrange for better resources next time. Perhaps some friends proved more helpful than others, and some of the rituals of sleeping and eating and lovemaking proved more productive than others. Nature may have become a special friend and music or art a staff for any tough journey. We can see where the journal helped, or psychotherapy, or grieving, just as we can see how helping others a bit, even when we were down, turned off the panic circuits. And we can afford to spend time figuring out our faith on new terms, deciding Who is in charge, and how, as well as where we must be counted on. What we want to keep from our inner travail we must also plan to give away, by a mysterious law of our days. So we must puzzle out what we can say, show, create, or call forth in particular others with whom we will not pose or patronize.

Dreams in the integration period may show us lists, draw diagrams, and chart directions, as Cayce often noted. Indeed, whatever is in consciousness may show up in the unconscious, even reasoned essays on creation and human nature. Not to know this and look for it would be to miss part of the gift of fresh archetypes or universal patterns.

Dreams may also identify or hint at precisely those who now need our support, as they labor with their own demons, whether such companions be young or old, near or far. Further, the dreams of the integration period may lead us into rooms of prayer, where the stillness makes us catch our breath when shafts of light slip past pillars. Because we are creatures of symbols, which includes rites, we may dream of invitations to baptisms, weddings, communal meals, and ordinations, as the dignity of our souls is conferred on us afresh when we rise from being knighted in our own Camelots. But dreams may just as well offer simple gifts that remind us of the whole shape of the growth episode or complex—a piece of fruit well ripened, or a path wending up a mountain, or the graceful shape of a pitcher.

In these eight stages—stylized and oversimplified, to be sure—we can see one of the greatest of human treasures: that program of deep growth built right into our natures, which knows what to do with challenges, including terrible crises. Now we can consider more closely how to draw forth new solutions and larger hearts from such hidden resources as Jung often guessed and Cayce tried to delineate, sometimes as karma, from his unusual perspective.

3

The Cayce Resource
for Personal Crisis

MOST OF US KNOW people, or know stories of them, who have responded to adversity with fresh solutions that helped both themselves and others. Such people are models from whom we can learn. They are not just examples of courage and perseverance, but guides to specific principles and strategies for growing through crisis.

Bill W., one of the cofounders of Alcoholics Anonymous (AA), turned his personal crisis into a life-restoring movement. One day, after years of incessant drinking, he found himself in a hospital bed. There he had a mystical experience that changed his life. When he left the hospital, he set forth to tell all his drinking friends about it, but got nowhere. Finally, instead of talking, he began to listen to others; he drew patience and understanding from his mystical encounter, and chose anonymity to avoid the egotism that had betrayed him. Soon the elements of the AA approach developed among fellow recovering alcoholics. This little piece of social invention has since transformed untold thousands of damaged lives.

Toyohiko Kagawa turned a personal crisis into a helpful invention. Before World War II, Kagawa was Japan's leading proponent of the rights of the poor in Tokyo, especially their needs for housing and medical care. This devout and immensely creative Christian was frequently jailed but found his own ways to use the dull time and the barren surroundings, as he told us.

One such extended incarceration, for example, left him with nothing but bare walls and a cell floor of pebbles. Laboriously he scratched out on one wall the complete periodic table of chemical elements known at that time, which he had previously memorized. Then he devised a game that young Japanese could play to learn it. The game proved so admirable and practical that Japanese educational authorities eventually adopted it and used it widely in schools.

Albert Schweitzer, the Swiss theologian and physician, felt he had to develop a medical mission in Lambaréné—a disease-ridden part of Africa—to help redress the exploitation of blacks and to express his philosophy of reverence for all life. He told us how he had created a crisis for himself by his move to the jungle.

Playing Bach on the organ was one of the deepest sources of his own faith and courage, and it had also made him one of the world's foremost interpreters of Bach. His concerts and recordings provided him with proceeds to help support his mission station. To his horror, in Lambaréné, jungle ants repeatedly ate up his beloved pianos. The crisis was made worse because his philosophy of life forbade him to exterminate the ants! Discouraged, and praying for help, he had the inspired inner vision to enclose his instrument in copper. With great effort, he succeeded in saving his piano without harming the ants. Schweitzer turned his personal crisis into ethical action to produce passages of beauty.

Sometimes those who come to the aid of a person in crisis also grow into new competence out of bitter trials. At a faculty party of a university with which we were associated, one professor told us the following story. It solved a riddle many on campus had sought to answer: Why did his department not only provide exceptional leadership for the faculty as a whole, but consistently draw the best students, have the highest morale, do forefront research, and land enviable grants?

A few years ago, he explained, a faculty member in the department had become severely mentally ill. When his hospitalization benefits ran out, he still required round-the-clock care. So without telling anyone (note the anonymity again!) the man's colleagues set up a work schedule, which they kept in the top drawer of the departmental secretary's desk. Every member of the department signed up, by ones or twos, to take a shift with their sorely troubled colleague in his small apartment. They told others only that he had a leave for illness, and never mentioned what they were doing. Day after day, night after night, they bore his verbal abuse, gave him his medication, fed him and read to him, sought to calm him, and restrained him from suicide—not for weeks, but for a year and a half. When he finally recovered, they simply announced that he had been away and put him back to work, taking no credit. But from that day on, the energy and ideas of the faculty and students in the department had taken off, and never stopped. These professors turned a crisis into a stream of vitality.

Edgar Cayce's extraordinary problem-solving activity appears to belong in a similar context. Although he did not invent his trance method for giving counsel, he knew what to do with it when it emerged, partly through disciplined Bible inquiry, and studying the lives of adventurous medical missionaries. These investigations had led him into a profound mystical experience with a radiant presence—of no special gender, he told us—that gave him his bearings when he sought guidance for others from beyond himself.

The context of Cayce's everyday waking creativity was also helpful to his discoveries, because his faith affirmed his assertion that there was always somewhere to start on a difficult problem, with God's help. This outlook in time drew him the friendship of many innovators (including Thomas Edison, who tried to record his readings, but could not figure out where to place the speaking tube without hampering the unconscious man). Cayce was himself an inventor. He found early in life that he could not play bridge, although he enjoyed it, because others concentrated so intensely that he could read their minds. So he invented other card games, such as the delightful Drinx. When he found the sun too hot to let him fish comfortably off the dock behind his house, he planted a tree in a caulked keg and floated it, so he could pull the shade anywhere he needed it.

And when he discovered that preteens in his Alabama Sunday school class were intimidated by the formal arrangement of chairs, he invented a horseshoe-shaped table that was often copied for the same purpose in other Southern churches.

Even as a young man, Cayce inspired people around him with the sense that they could do something about hopeless circumstances. His first Sunday school class for young adults at Ninth Street Christian Church in Hopkinsville, Kentucky, drew thirty-eight members, of which *half* ended up going abroad to places like Africa and Tibet as medical missionaries. Cayce turned his own stresses and challenges into creations and faith that refreshed and inspired others.

THE CAYCE RESOURCE FOR GROWING THROUGH CRISIS

Edgar Cayce had only a grade-school education, but he was an avid student of life. His creations far outstripped his conscious resources. His life work decisively poses to the rest of us the question of how to find creative solutions to daunting or crippling circumstances.

To be sure, Cayce was self-taught in the content and complex import of the Bible, which he memorized almost entirely. He was richly tutored by his thousands of readings, as well as reasonably informed in many areas of current affairs by his good mind and active church life. But he exhibited a remarkable ability to come up with workable solutions to the baffling and often life-threatening problems brought to him by people from many walks of life. Usually their problems, because they were medical, involved crises. But he also dealt with other difficult challenges: vocational, spiritual, business, and even criminal.

Cayce's trance discourses provide a view of soul growth across centuries. They present a version of reincarnation (discussed in detail in chapter six) that views debilitating hardships and crises as meaningful karma encountered on the way to full companionship with God. Cayce's counsel provided individuals with such illuminating detail of past and future lives that this worldview became for many an option in serious Christian faith (the first time this had happened on any significant scale since the Alexandrian school of Clement and Origen in Egypt, during the third century). Later Cayce's view and that of others—including Carl Jung, according to his biographer, Laurens Van der Post—helped to stimulate a considerable movement in American life toward rethinking human nature and destiny. A recent opinion survey by the Gallup organization, reported in *Emerging Trends* by the Princeton Religious Research Center, indicates that about one American in four now considers reincarnation a reality.

How did Cayce suggest that we work with our crises, as he himself did with his calamities, to achieve real transformation of selfhood and society? To answer this question we must consider the four elements of the total Cayce resource: the man, the gift, the concepts, and the consequent responses of people and groups drawn to his story and worldview.

The Man

The first component of the Cayce legacy is the man himself. Edgar Cayce was not otherworldly, as he is sometimes pictured. He was a man who traveled widely, read newspapers and magazines, liked good food, appreciated attractive women, and loved to fish and garden. He also took his lumps in running not only photographic studios in several cities, but a sizable petroleum company doing its own drilling, a full-fledged busy hospital, and a nonprofit research organization. He was not a fundamentalist, and did not insist on rigid views of biblical events and biblical authorship. He was profoundly influenced by the biblical saga of the human journey with God, and found in Jesus not only a theological norm but a living friend.

Cayce is often described as simple, plain, and humble. However, what makes his life exciting and relevant to many is precisely that he was *not* simple, as his own readings on himself pointed out. He was as complicated and tension-ridden as most of us. Many-sided in his artistic, inventive, theological, poetic, and healing talents, he had to ride himself at the same time he rode his special trance gift. By determined discipline, he kept to a plain and unpretentious life, never exploiting his gift and refusing to advertise it. But the effort stretched him to his limits, for he was inclined to worry often and long about not having enough money. He wondered whether he was entitled to solve crimes for rewards, locate lost silver mines, invest in stocks, discover pirate treasure, or drill into hidden oil deposits—all of which he briefly tried, with no success for himself or backing for his medical work, but with sometimes startling success for others. He was a proud man, deferring to none. Yet his deep love of God made him able to love God's people, one by one, so genuinely that his handyman, the man who delivered his eggs, and a vice president of the United States each felt free to call on his unusual aid and friendship.

Cayce's readings were not simply paranormal knowledge. They were just as truly expressions of deep human values, brought to bear on the crises presented to him. His readings can properly be seen as a high order of person-empowering love in action. This is evidenced not only by their literal content, but by their place in the flow of Cayce's articulate and concerned letters, phone calls, and visits with sufferers, as well as in his prayers for them. Relevant, too, was his generosity with readings. In his earlier years, he charged nothing; and even at the end of his life he gave away a fifth of his readings to people who found even twenty dollars too steep to pay in wartime.

The full dimensions of this kind of labor are obscured by the notion of his contributions as "information." They are also obscured by the too-simple preoccupation with mimicking his techniques for "channeling" in altered states of consciousness, rather than attempting the heartfelt commitments he made and shared. Cayce's total aid process can be described as "love surprised by wisdom." If we are to learn from Cayce how to handle crises, we must keep the man in view as a corrective to oversimplifying what he did and said.

The Gift

The second component of the Cayce resource is his remarkable gift in action. Although his trance ability seems far beyond most of our daily lives, it was part of the creativity that imbued everything he undertook—his play and his spirituality, his teaching and his friendships. It was not accidental to such a way of life that he developed one night, for a Y.M.C.A. event, a game called "Pit" or "Corner the Market," which has been played by generations of Americans ever since. In addition, his camera studies won prizes across the South for their artistry. Innovative problem solving was for him a way of life. Many suspect it was this ability that made his unusual readings possible, because it reinforced an essential array of formative archetypes for his counsel.

Such inventive living is by no means out of reach of the rest of us. To find new solutions to crises from Cayce's example, we have to pay attention to the stages and modifiers of his central creative act and to its conditions, as shown by his successes and failures. Unfortunately, the responses of most of those he helped were not recorded, so this kind of investigation is not easy. We are often stuck with only his transcribed side of counseling transactions—which may be highly suggestive, but hardly authoritative. Most of those who sought his aid are now dead. We can properly attempt as research only validation of his apparent hypotheses by scholarship, experiment, and individual "application"—a term much used in his trance material. Again, describing the literal contents of his readings as "information" can be misleading and irresponsible, if it is meant to suggest bona fide tested findings and not raw data.

Fortunately, a generation of psychologists and theorists of religion has been hard at work since his death. Today we can find what appear to be instructive parallels to much of what Cayce did in giving his counsel, especially in the study of dreams. There our consciousness may be free to discover surprising solutions that parallel the workings of his trance—just as his readings suggested.

We all want easy answers, and may be tempted to find them too quickly in Cayce. It is important to remember that his counsel was adamant that his ideas should be shared "never on authority," but always as subject to testing and modification.

He is also reported as intending to share his readings with everyone through this vehicle. But that account is misleading. Cayce was not out to be a guru, or to create a vehicle for a mass following of his teachings. Instead, he was committed to fostering responsible inquiry by professionals working in their own communities of disciplined research and thought. He felt it was up to them to gain a wider hearing for whatever they might find valuable in his readings and in comparative phenomena and concepts. To that end, in 1931, his friends founded the Association for Research and Enlightenment (A.R.E.), to give him room to conduct his necessarily experimental readings, as well as to facilitate responsible research on these and related materials.

We live in a world of shifting values, and large institutions that seem beyond our control. It may comfort us, when we are in personal crisis, to find in someone like Cayce—or Emanuel Swedenborg in the past, or the Maharishi or Reverend Moon in the present, or Ramtha or Emmanuel or Seth or some other trance source—what appear to be answers for all sorts of questions, ready for consumption in the company of like-minded believers. But this is the path to a Cayce cult, and directly violates the manner in which his gift was exercised. His readings strenuously warned against making the Cayce resource into a "sect, schism, or ism," offering teachings on private, untested authority. Such an outcome creates children, not adults.

We may properly look to Cayce's well-documented gift—not unfailingly accurate, but still remarkably consistent in its helpfulness for forty years—to find clues to our own capacities for fresh solutions to tough problems. It is not irrelevant to note that Cayce often insisted, "I don't do anything you can't do, if you are willing to pay the price."

The Concepts

The concepts—the systematic ideas and practical strategies found in Cayce's readings—range over a wide array of topics. They include not only advice about unusual and intractable medical disorders (because people so often came to Cayce as a last resort), but treatments not always orthodox or likely. Other subjects run the gamut from ancient societies and astrology to the nature of God and the layers of the psyche. Yet Cayce's thought is not available in orderly essays developed in long readings given for that purpose. He gave his attention directly to individuals in need, rather than creating a total system that carefully specified central and peripheral matters. As a result, many have picked up items from his readings and presented them as representing Cayce's thought, without having to show how these relate to his central concepts and intents.

In our society (which already trivializes weighty matters by such practices as giving denture cleaners equal time with the most sobering of nightly news), it is easy to present Cayce's ideas as a counter display of colorful items: soul mates, lucid dreams, fragments of Atlantis, eating almonds to prevent cancer, communicating with plants, gathering in groups that study and pray, sojourns in other realms of consciousness than earth, wearing crystals, and the redemptive work of the Christ may all be laid out indiscriminately for the picking.

In our eagerness to use these items, we may forget to question their validity for ourselves. We may also lose sight of the seriousness of human evil, both individual and collective, which is evident in his readings, and the imperative to loving personal and social change that is strong in both the Cayce counsel and his life. Yet the determined seeker after insight about crises can sort through the jumble and find some patterns of meaning. Using the Cayce resource well requires persistent study to separate the serious from the merely strange; drawing on comparative materials (such as the works of Carl Jung); and checking the concepts against the factual reality of Cayce's life and gift.

The concepts themselves are embedded in some 14,000 remaining transcripts (thousands of readings went unrecorded for twenty years). These often-sophisticated individual readings contain three kinds of statements: postulates, covariations, and prescriptions.

Postulates.   Some statements offer key *postulates* or constructs in Cayce's thought—about the body, the psyche, history, the heavens, or something else. Examples of such notions include the soul, karma, vibrations, and the Creative Forces. They are the basic playing pieces on the board of Cayce's thought, and as such they require no immediate direct proof. Yet the final intent of any system such as his is to generate proof of the value of just such postulates, for explaining and predicting empirical data. These constructs need to be clearly specified as to their operation and interaction, lest they turn into well-meant garble. Comparison with other key concepts in systems like or unlike Cayce's is essential for clarity and depth, as he himself so often modeled in trance by comparing his concepts with biblical thought, William James, or Lao-Tzu.

Covariations. Cayce's readings also offer *covariations*, or correlations among observable processes and experiences. We all learned in school that "If X is done under Y conditions, then Z will result." If we meditate, dreams will get clearer. If we forgive others, we can better forgive ourselves. But the discoveries in our lives are rarely that simple. Here we begin to play the game with the specified pieces in earnest, and we start to discover whether the postulates for Cayce's system are workable or faulty. Evidence of many kinds, direct and indirect, is now absolutely essential. Simply announcing that correlations are true, either because they sound probable or came from Cayce, is irresponsible.

Prescriptions. Finally, there are *prescriptions*, or instructions. They are proffered in Cayce's readings because they have repeatedly been derived, or can be derived, from tested covariations. Osteopathy should be used to treat mental illness. Intercourse should be limited to marriage. Such statements may appear because someone ill is in a tremendous hurry and needs the best that Cayce can suggest, right then and no nonsense, with proof to come later. Cayce in trance often had to speak in such terms, or try to teach individuals about meditation or dream interpretation or the prevention of illness without restating to each person all over again his basic or systematic concepts. Thus many statements in his readings are of this prescriptive type. However, they may not be parroted—except in emergencies, for good and temporary reasons—unless the speaker or writer can suggest how independent verification has been attempted, with what results, and in what manner others can replicate. (All of these distinctions apply just as well to Jung's thought, or the thought of any other systematic author or counselor. It is tempting to jump over them because of the unusual nature of Cayce's discourse. For example, had Jung made all his statements in a strange ancient tongue, or from beyond the grave, instead of in books with impressive scholarship and the sharp criticism of colleagues in responsible communities of inquiry, we might have had to review the rules for him in the same way. Such communities are in short supply for Cayce.)

All the warnings about care in using Cayce's concepts carry a further dimension of caution, expressed by this quote from many of his readings: "Knowledge not lived is sin." Cayce's thought carries an existential note, insisting that we only really know what we try out in daily life, and that which we pronounce without that testing can be hollow, misleading, or destructive egotism. The image we have used above of games and playing pieces falls short of this gravity in Cayce's concepts.

People and Groups Responsive to Cayce

The fourth component of the total Cayce resource is the response to his work shown by those individual lives and organizational programs that have tried to work carefully and persistently with the other three components. It would hardly be fair to Cayce to saddle his life and thought with all that others have done and said about him in his name. Yet one test of a body of thought is its consequences in real life. Karl Marx without communism would be an incomplete study, as would Freud without analysis. Using this element of the Cayce resource is partly a task for biographers and historians. But insofar as groups and programs continue to announce that they are Cayce-based, it is reasonable to see in them either illuminating consequences of his concepts and efforts, or a challenge to specify how they may have distorted his heritage.

Publications and programs that draw on Cayce are not widespread, yet they are varied and helpful. Dozens of books have been written about him and his readings. Courses on Cayce's thought are taught in adult education programs of a number of community colleges (usually not for credit). One Presbyterian seminary has offered a graduate credit course on Cayce, Jung, and Steiner for many years. Mainline churches, some of them leaders in their denominations, as well as those of New Thought persuasion, have sponsored groups studying Cayce's concepts, and practicing Cayce-inspired disciplines of service and spiritual growth. A few research centers, including the Mayo Clinic, have investigated selected aspects of Cayce's thought; we have been called on to consult in such ventures. Businesses, large and small, have made some deliberate use of consultants familiar with the Cayce resource. Although no university center sponsors regular projects on his hypotheses, so far as we have been able to find out, a course on Cayce has been offered for some years to trainees at the C. G. Jung Institut in Switzerland. Spiritual Frontiers Fellowship has offered occasional lectures and workshops on Cayce to its national lay membership, for three decades.

It is natural for those interested in Cayce's life, gift, and thought to turn to organizations chiefly concerned with it. The one that parallels most closely his medical aid to individuals is the A.R.E. Medical Clinic in Phoenix, Arizona. Developed over several decades under the leadership of a husband-and-wife team of medical doctors, William and Gladys McGarey, the clinic has been highly influential in the emergence of the American Holistic Medical Association (A.M.H.A.), composed of several thousand physicians. Cayce theories and remedies are central, but treatment is not limited to these. The clinic has a large staff of physicians and other health professionals representing a range of disciplines. Like Cayce, they take on one sufferer at a time, using multifaceted processes that encourage patients to use their own dreams as readings on their conditions. The clinic also sponsors an annual symposium of medical pioneers, publishes a medical bulletin and a newsletter, trains interns, conducts foundation-sponsored research, and reaches out to other groups of professionals that are exploring the Cayce legacy. It has developed its own considerable lore of ways to deal with life-threatening crises, which is not limited to medical aspects. Considering the nature and work of this clinic is a reasonable step in evaluating the total Cayce resource, and useful for keeping its other components in perspective.

A much larger and completely separate organization has developed in Cayce's home community of Virginia Beach, Virginia: the Association for Research and Enlightenment, often called A.R.E. This pioneering organization has taken a very different tack over the forty years since Cayce's death. It has welcomed and assisted a number of medical researchers, but has felt constrained chiefly to build a sizable national lay membership, now approaching a hundred thousand. This health-psychological-spiritual interest group has in the past defined itself in various ways, most often as a vehicle for psychic research. Today it offers resources to members and the public on a wide spectrum of topics related in some degree to those in the Cayce readings.

Unlike Cayce, who avoided publicity after painful experiences with it, and who never advertised his work, this organization has understandably advertised and promoted vigorously. It has developed a membership magazine, a press, extensive mail-order book sales, a library and conference center, lectures and seminars in scores of cities, a summer camp, a network of study groups, overseas tours, some research projects largely funded by participants, and the beginnings of an accredited university. Since many of its constituents are people confronted by or recovering from personal crises, the work of this enterprise deserves careful attention.

Perhaps even more important for understanding and using the full Cayce resource are the life stories of those who have systematically tried to engage the fourfold Cayce legacy in their lives. Little study has yet been made of these. As might be expected, some have found life-renewing help, while others have selected only remedies or skills or books and moved on. Some have developed from Cayce's legacy an entire way of life that is often in contrast to mainstream culture, with its own groups, rites, and vocabulary. Our purpose here will be to suggest approaches to the total Cayce resource, which our experience has shown to have lasting value for anyone who is confronting a severe life crisis. Our intent is to stimulate personal exploration, not to win adherents to a group or trend.

THE CAYCE RESOURCE AND CURRENT SOCIAL MOVEMENTS

The thoughtful reader will inevitably try to understand Cayce by bracketing him with like viewpoints and phenomena, recognizing that the several components of the Cayce resource may point in differing directions. For the individual grappling with distressing or crippling personal crisis, this kind of judgment is serious, because most of us tend to look further in the direction in which we are helped. Yet few of life's experiences are as cruel as discovering that a solution to a life-shattering blow is not a solution at all, but a shallow distraction.

Is the Cayce legacy representative of the amorphous but vigorous movement of thought and practice called New Age? *Time* left out Cayce entirely in a lengthy cover story on the phenomenon. Yet several themes that early appeared in discussions of a New Age are prominent in Cayce's thought. The earth, matter, and flesh have been revisioned by New Age advocates to assign them "psychoid" or psyche-like properties. One result has been fresh approaches to ecological concerns, holistic health, psychic experiences, and planetary peace and productivity. Women, long associated with matter and the body in Western thought and faith, got a hearing that not only redefined social roles but presented both sexes with the challenge of rebalancing their yin and yang qualities. At the same time, mind and consciousness got called up for overhaul in the New Age movement. Exploration of altered states showed staggering reaches of awareness in ordinary people. The concept of reincarnation offered to stretch the boundaries of identity and destiny. Affirmations and other methods of controlling one's attitudes became more appealing when the threat of uncontrolled nuclear devastation hung in the air. Finally, the very nature of social and personal change came up for review, whether seen in "paradigm shifts" or in the slow parade of astrological epochs.

For all of these themes, parallels in Cayce's thought may be found. Yet the center of the Cayce view of personal and social change is clearly a focus on a God-initiated process that he called "the coming of the Christ" into human affairs. This theme is easily buried in New Age dreamy music, reports of consciousness-expansion by celebrities, expensive readings by those channeling cosmic or Atlantean masters, crystals, seminars on firewalking, and astrological guidance for business or government. Far from Cayce, too, is a focus on self-development and personal success at the expense of justice or service for those in pain and hardship. The discerning reader must judge how to frame the extraordinary Cayce resource in the various categories of our times.

CREATING NEW SOLUTIONS TO PERSONAL CRISIS

Cayce had little reason to doubt that forces far beyond his own could help him aid others, though they could not help him meet contrived and self-willed demands. Twice a day he entered a trance state preceded by prayer. This trance seemed in some ways more an extension of his prayer than a result of conventional hypnosis. In this state, he found he could pluck from the minds of sick people, even when they were far from him, exact descriptions of their limbs, organ systems, mental states, infections, injuries, and medical histories. He could do all this in such detail that physicians willing to consider his report (not all would) could usually verify his diagnosis and history for themselves (thought not all did).

Further, he found that he could pluck from sources unknown to him a complex array of treatments that repeatedly led the blind to see, the lame to walk, the deaf to hear, the psychotic to sanity, and the diseased to health. He could even specify instantly where little-known remedies could be located, in any part of the country, just as he could locate treatment devices or programs in physiotherapy or electrotherapy. In his trance, he could specify ways to compound effective new drugs, as well as describe delicate new treatment appliances. Just as swiftly, he could name the best physician in the country to treat a difficult condition. Even more astonishing, he could steer a patient to a physician just down the person's street—though the location was unfamiliar to Cayce, who was a thousand miles away or farther.

In later years, Cayce found he could pull forth comparably effective vocational and psychological guidance. He also turned in these years to business guidance; he limited this, however, because it often left a residue of power strivings in his psyche that upset him. In addition, he inspected historical events for scholars, and facilitated inventions for engineers.

Conditions of the Cayce Resource

It is important to recognize that Cayce's process had limits. *He could not make decisions for others*. They needed to make decisions for themselves—whether on a troubled marriage, a career opportunity, an impulse to join or avoid the military, a desire to serve the needy, or even whether to help Cayce in his treatment or research efforts. Cayce's sources had immense respect for the worth of individuals, as he did; they required individuals to make their own requests for aid, as well as to use their own free will and judgment to determine the course of their lives. Cayce could supply resources, and point out implications and perspectives, but his counsel was resolutely person-building. It did not seek or allow Cayce devotees.

He could not exploit the needs of others, nor help them to exploit their fellows. If he tried, his counsel would be refused in trance. When he attempted to use it in questionable areas, his counsel could make mistakes (as it did when he tried to specify Texas oil deposits for some investors whose greed seemed to exceed his own more idealistic desire to fund a hospital).

He could not give his aid at the expense of his own health, or allow others to use him in directions of which he did not approve. The result would be painful headaches, or falling into unconsciousness for an involuntary rest, or just having nothing come forth in trance.

THE CAYCE RESOURCE AT WORK IN A MODERN CLINIC

It is tempting to focus on Cayce as a remarkable figure of the past, overlooking the many processes for creative problem solving and the transforming of personhood that he both exemplified and explained for those in crisis. The work of the A.R.E. Clinic today in Phoenix, Arizona, offers a useful corrective. Here one may see a staff of nearly forty physicians and support personnel committed to seeking Cayce-like intuitive and psychic guidance of their own. They are also committed to eliciting similar leads from patients, as they join dreams, hunches, and prayer to thorough conventional medical diagnoses and treatment regimens. They draw on the rich Cayce medical resource, but only with critical professional discrimination, and join to it a variety of other therapies.

The clinic has shown phenomenal success—though certainly not universal—for over two decades, as it has taken on persons in crises precipitated by cancer, brain injury, birth defects, AIDS, advanced heart disease, multiple sclerosis, severe arthritis, psychosis, depression, suicidal tendencies, and many other medical ailments. Some of those it has helped through shattering crises are not sick but instead wounded by death loss, or handicapped by vocational or spiritual confusion.

The genius of the clinic (which it has systematically shared with others in the holistic health movement) lies in recognizing that "all healing comes from within," as Cayce suggested. Accordingly, high priority is given to fostering deep archetypal growth as central to recovery. Patients are helped to take responsibility for their own lives, and to enrich their relations with the divine, by processes that match the vigor of needed medical and surgical interventions. A healing community in a gracious setting is formed by putting a dozen sufferers from diverse ailments together for ten to seventeen days of rich personal sharing and mutual support. The potent group field that results grows with daily telling of the life stories of participants, enhanced by attention to dreams, at meals that become quiet feasts of hope. Humor and play are joined to meditation and thoughtful seminars on health principles as the pain-cramped and initially guarded sufferers venture into easy movements of dance, and then into drawing with music, encountering nature, and spontaneously celebrating gains. Massage provides tender care, while biofeedback and imaging teach how to help the body and mind do their natural healing work.

What happens again and again to those in threatening crises is not only renewed health, but released fear, and quickened compassion. Fresh designs for love, work, and faith are also prompted. Those who come as victims of crippling blows leave as creators, agents of their own futures.

4

How to Become
Agents of Change

How can we become agents of needed change, not just victims? The answer to this question is the heart of growing through crisis. In this chapter, we will look at some major components of the Cayce view, best explored by wider reading, and by trying out perspectives and procedures with a journal and good companions.

CHOOSE TO BE A COCREATOR

The first condition for participating in the Cayce process is to choose to be a cocreator: to work not only with others, but always with the divine. Our solutions to crises must empower others as well as ourselves. In them, we must aim for richer loving, more cooperative and imaginative productivity, more risk-taking and pain-handling stature—in ways that will keep right on bearing good fruit. Our solutions need to be both practical and liberating. They must meet needed ends, but should also be graceful, honest, and just.

The Cayce readings view human destiny in these terms: we will become increasing cocreators with the Creator, who called each soul into life at the beginning. In such an approach, not all of our wishes or desires will find fulfillment. A dying or dead child may not necessarily be revived, a lost lover reembraced, a shattered business reclaimed, or a betrayed cause repaired.

In a cocreating approach, our first question must be "God, what would you have me do and be?", not "How can I get what I want right now?" More often than not, a humble spirit and a contrite heart, pledged to cocreating with the One, will find resources where none seemed possible. Whether the final outcome is enduring loss with an uncomplaining spirit distilled to loveliness, or developing a sudden fresh solution to a seemingly insoluble problem; whether it be turning in a radically new direction for unguessed developments, or the slow achievement of stature such that one's tree will shade other sufferers; the God on whom Cayce felt he drew could be trusted to hear and respond to those who sought in trust and patience to be cocreators.

Such a lifestyle—which constantly seeks solutions fruitful both for others and oneself, and responsive to a larger will—can spring into action from the cries of any of us. It will develop best when we cultivate it over time, with steady resolve. Cayce's readings urged everyone to work with explicit ideals—writing them down and rephrasing them in a prayerful spirit attuned by the company of large-spirited persons, whether these be found in scriptures or literature or in one's friends and colleagues. Such ideals are not goals or objectives, not time-bound targets to reach (though these have their place), but the emblazoned colors and heraldry of the soul.

Here Cayce departed from the ways of some New Thought and "metaphysical" devotees, who advise us to visualize whatever immediate prosperity, relationships, or benefits we want from the universe, and insist that they be manifested. Cayce's readings agreed, over and over, that thoughts were immensely powerful in determining events—not only by shaping the thinker, but by drawing unseen forces or "vibrations" and "thought forms" into play to enhance desirable outcomes. But the formula Cayce offered went beyond manipulating consciousness: "The Spirit is the life, mind is the builder, and the physical is the result." For the mind to get the physical results it is bountifully equipped to bring about, the desired ends need to be grounded in and often reshaped by the Spirit—known not only intuitively, but in company with other seekers, using disciplined reason and the witness of a large spiritual tradition.

Defining Ideals

Cayce's readings often advised people to define their ideals. To do this, select a piece of paper and draw two vertical lines. Set down "My Ideal" in three columns of lists and phrases—one apiece for spiritual, mental, and physical. This is meant to be an ongoing process. It requires much erasing and replacing by items more positive, more concrete, more outgoing; you will have to integrate the ideals in one column with ideals that support and implement them in the others. Always, the enterprise of fashioning ideals for a cocreating life needs to be grounded in a sense of what one's deepest thinking and intuitions suggest God wants from one's particular talents and circumstances.

Once the ideal-making process is set in motion, it can be reinforced by drawings, chosen symbols, and sharing with others. The next task is to set the mind and spirit going—thinking up ways to express the ideals in particular situations. The readings encourage playfulness, imagination, curiosity, and possibility-thinking. They tell us we will have difficulty attaining what we have not yet thought of, though God is the Surpriser, ever bringing gifts we do not know enough to ask for. The little-understood processes of the psychic area need a cultivated imagination in touch with living archetypes, in order to get fresh paranormal impressions or to send forth the helpful energies that the soul surmises are fitting.

In Cayce's view, severe problems typically carry elements of their own solutions: suffering activates archetypes or "patterns"; hardship sensitizes us to others, whose aid or needs might be overlooked; pain fires the nerves and emotions to higher levels of motivation and imagination. Every "stumbling block" is potentially a "stepping stone" to better solutions, larger personhood, or both. In a daring extension of this view, which affirms the loving care or providence offered to each individual, the Cayce readings insist that nobody is tested beyond what he or she can bear. This astonishing claim, which many in the midst of suffering would find unbelievable, rests in part on a deeper view of the interface between events and personhood, where circumstance is discerned and felt as loss in proportion to one's inner capacity to respond and seek aid. But it also mirrors a universe more purposeful and fair than most of us imagine (as we shall see in chapter six, when we consider the workings of karma).

A COCREATING COVENANT

The next step is to set resources into motion by promises or covenants. In the Cayce view, God has already made promises of support and guidance that are worth digging out of scriptures and mining from one's own spiritual experiences and quiet times. "I will not leave you comfortless" (from 14:18 in the Gospel of John) is one of these; so is the assurance, "If you will be my people, I will be your God" (found in Exodus 19:5 and elsewhere); and "the Spirit itself beareth witness with our spirit" (from Paul's soaring letter to the Romans, 8:16).

Again and again Cayce urged those who sought his help and wanted to learn a way of cocreating to discover what was already in motion in the universe on their behalf, by studying such promises and working with their implications in daily life. The God spoken of here is not an indulgent daddy, or a potentate granting favors for fawning. This God is a creator, finding joy in the creations of his/her people, and in their own aspirations and promises made in turn. So a primary condition for creating new solutions is to make one's own commitments to the divine—as religious traditions have always undertaken in the use of vows, and literature such as *Faust* tells in accounts of pacts made either with God or with Mephistopheles.

Part of making a covenant is to seek ways to be more fully alive and effective. This must be done in accordance with the ideals you have already worked on. Cayce's readings note that establishing disciplined and compelling ideals, transparent to the will of the divine, is the most important step a soul can take. Without these, everything else can falter or go awry. Ask boldly for talents, for opportunities, for associates, for resources, but always in a willing, cocreating spirit that promises how and where they will be used.

Many able people can miss the help the universe proffers to them in distress, because they forget to ask, but wait instead to be struck by destiny or pulled out of sulks and fears. To ask and promise in some nobility requires us to specify, as far as we can get it clear by persistent seeking, just which people and groups will be given the outcomes. Merely asking for self-enhancement will not work, because it is an incomplete circuit. One must weigh, as did Moses before the burning bush, and Jesus in prayer before facing crucifixion, "Who are my people?" Whom did I come into this life to be accountable to, and to serve? What ages, circumstances, ideals, talents, education, and needs mark these, my people? Whom am I most needed by and suited to aid and to celebrate?

Such covenants also require us to promise to pay the price of whatever talents or circumstances we seek: learning new skills or concepts, being willing to fail and try again, putting aside needless distractions and negative stimuli or companions, growing into unfamiliar sides of selfhood, and readiness to start with whatever is at hand. Nothing short of what Søren Kierkegaard called "willing one thing" in this whole-souled way can bring the fullest results; yet that will always has to be checked against the larger will of God. What we seek in deep intent must be the best we know. The Creator, in the account of the Cayce readings, seeks fully adult companions, not just well-behaved children. "Don't be goody-goody," was often the counsel, "be good *for* something."

To make a serious promise implies accountability. Confession and repentance, as well as admission of limitations, are as real in the Cayce worldview as they are in AA. One needs to be bold and take risks, or God cannot bring helpful energies to bear. "Better to be doing something, even if it is wrong," was Cayce's counsel. It was not meant to advise haste or impulsiveness, but to challenge people to step beyond that guardedness, that defensiveness, that passivity which is finally sin because it entails hiding from God. Yet he put "Empty self if you would be filled" right beside the injunction to step out on the best one knew. As in Jung's thought, the reconciling of necessary opposites is an essential process in all of Cayce's counsel.

Since humans are social beings, our covenants should not be a private engagement of God. Promises made best are offered before people we cherish, as we do wedding vows (though not necessarily as formally). We must do our private work with journals and reading and decision making, but we must also take steps in public, before those pledged to like ideals and accountability. We can draw witnesses and companions from family or friends; or from fellow seekers, committed to one another and God within a tradition larger than themselves, which could both fructify their resolve and challenge it when needed.

SEEKING FULL SELFHOOD

Covenants require real people filled with juice and fire and principle, not shadowy spiritual devotees. To make this clear, Cayce's readings spelled out for individuals their rich resources of temperament and drives, gender and talents, hang-ups and heroism, in what were called "life readings." But the concept of seeking full selfhood was there even in medical counsel, where people were told, "So live that you can look anyone in the eye and tell them where to go!" As creations of the divine itself, which longed for such comradeship, selves or souls were incredibly precious. They were given centuries and huge free will to realize their potential and common destiny. (We will explore this further in the discussion of reincarnation in chapter six.)

The Cayce counsel constantly warns against corrosive self-attack and self-condemnation, seeing these as belittling that dream of the Creator which each soul is. Many guilts and faults are real and destructive, requiring naming and purging; Cayce's readings never blink at sin, personal or social. But human beings too often arrogate to themselves judging that cuts the nerve of resolve and leads them to hide from the divine, as Adam and Eve did in the primal Garden. The Cayce picture of human nature does not start with natural depravity, though it includes a concept of the Fall by rebelliousness in which all actually and individually participated. Yet even as it affirms that "All have sinned and fallen short," his counsel invites a firm "nevertheless" that comes with putting one's whole trust in God.

Most of us learn as adults that when we condemn others we become vulnerable to using the same harsh standards on ourselves, or drawing such judgments on our heads from others. The Cayce readings warn that "magnifying agreements, minimizing faults" in others is essential for cocreators. Each of us is required to tame the tongue, modify the runaway mood, if we want to stand where the light of inspiration can strike us. Hot anger in the agony of grief is one thing, always forgivable; but persistent blaming and hidden rage can only poison the body and mind.

Cayce pointed out both debilitating fatigue and crippling fear as traps. Indeed, the Cayce source traces mental illness (after first addressing physiological problems) to runaway fear and doubt. Cayce's outlook asks us to stand tall, secure in the love of God, which we can know intimately by trying to give it away to others. In this view, there is no need to exaggerate our problems as a means of self-terrorizing, nor to bluff by undervaluing our problems. Quiet realism and earnest trust will do, even if it means staying awake in Gethsemane's garden while all our friends sleep.

Having tested our ideals, and entered into pledged covenants, we can risk all, offer all passion and direction, toward the best we know, confident that failures will be forgiven and poor efforts redirected. "Know that the try is counted for righteousness" was a theme often repeated in the Cayce counsel to encourage getting started, beginning with whatever is at hand. If we are not willing to fail, we are probably also unwilling to succeed, secretly guarding against new responsibilities.

Real inventiveness and leadership means releasing concern for credit, in the assurance that "God looks on the heart" and that "Nothing truly ours can ever be lost." And when the time comes for honest regret over things done or left undone, we can rest in the assurance that "Nothing is ever over": the soul continues to draw wisdom and courage and love from all the corners of its experience, good and bad, and to transform the unworthy into new ventures for which whole lifetimes are appointed.

ATTUNEMENT AND SERVICE

From the Cayce readings emerge two great and familiar commandments for human unfolding: "loving God with all the heart, mind, soul, and strength," and "loving one's neighbor as oneself." When these are kept in steady balance, all other growth will develop as needed. Because temperaments differ, that balance will not always be easy. Some in troubled times hasten to step aside, pray and meditate, garner the treasures of nature and the arts, wander the inner world of wonders, be troubadours of God. All of this attunement and much more is appropriate, and indeed essential for the delicate connections called psychic or prophetic or inspired. But it does little good and builds no lasting personhood unless it is firmly connected to meeting the needs of others—not in stylized charity, but in hearty collaboration, as service.

Other individuals might be tempted to neglect attunement, seeking instead to be busy with good works, great projects, or enterprises of ego masked as service. To keep such efforts more sensitive and fruitful, better timed and aimed, requires regular attunement—not only to God, but to one's fellows and to the rest of creation, as well as to graceful forms. Only that service or sturdy building led "by cloud and by fire," discerned in devotion, can fully be trusted; for the two great commandments belong together.

According to Cayce, a cocreating lifestyle is more than the intent of ideals and the pledges of covenants, made in confident self-affirmation. What keeps all these real and workable is the gentle alternation between attunement and service, in a life as ready to muse as to manufacture, to bless as to build, to wait as to will.

THE ANATOMY OF INSPIRATION: THE CHAKRAS

Cayce's stream of thought was so earnestly and freely biblical in theme and illustration, that many were surprised to find one of the central concepts in his readings using the language of Hindu and Tibetan kundalini yoga. This system of concepts postulates streams of energy within and about each person, operating in all our creativity—from the most obvious forms of procreation to the most elusive forms of thinking, praying, and dying for others. In the Cayce view, the same circuits (involving not only nerves, but the potent endocrine glands) are employed in both attunement and service. He felt it crucial that the West study and understand them, as well as apply them.

Cayce presented a pattern of two energies meeting: each ultimately drawn from the divine, but given differing and complementary forms. One is the natural creative vitality or spirit of the individual. It is shaped by the soul and directed by the mind, but is also expressed in the flesh and life force; this is done in part through a "finer body" visible only to psychic perception, as in auras. The other is the Spirit of the divine or universal or Creative Forces, ever ready to respond to the individual's own energy, adding thrust and wisdom and love to it, as needed. The dance of the two energies is conducted through seven swirling *chakras* (the Sanskrit term for wheel) or *centers*. The chakras are said to engage the flesh in a sequence that stretches from the vital gonads; up through a focal area in the lower abdomen concerned with yin and yang energies; upward to the forcefulness of anger and fear and courage in the adrenal or belly area; and then to the chest or "heart," the seat of feelings and interpersonal caring. From there the energy flows to the three "higher" centers: one at the throat, specially concerned with will; one at the forehead, concerned with the best creations and with fullest personhood; and one at the crown of the head, concerned with illumination of mind and memory. (Traditional Eastern sources give variant views, but this is the Cayce version.)

According to Cayce, the kundalini path is implanted in all as a birthright. In this way, creative energy can rise from its origins in the great coiled snake of the gonads, travel through the centers, and be met by the Spirit of the divine at the crown of the head or pineal center—just where the waters of the Ganges fall on Shiva, or the early Christians found tongues of fire on Pentecost, and many today encounter force, as well as trembling and blessing. Then the aroused formative energy, rich with archetypal quality, circulates down again, blessing all the great motors of motivation and striving that are built into the flesh.*

---

*It should be noted firmly that this scheme has been relatively little studied or carefully researched in the West, although versions exist in Theosophical literature and its variant, Anthroposophy, developed by Rudolph Steiner. So in setting forth the Cayce picture for use in seeking creative solutions to crises, we can only explore hypotheses, not established material. However, we have worked with this framework for forty years, and found it useful for tracking and empowering many kinds of inventiveness and inspiration, as well as healing energies.

THE EIGHT PHASES OF INSPIRATION

The following phases of the process of inspiration are modeled loosely on the Cayce kundalini perspective. They provide a scheme for working with natural resources to find creative solutions during times of stress and crisis. These phases may often be telescoped, so that one is absorbed into others. Indeed, the whole process may take place in minutes or hours; or it may require slow emergence over weeks or months.

It is helpful to keep a journal to record and analyze experiences, and to compare them with those of others—whether in literature, biography, or among associates. Paying attention to dream symbols that pace the kundalini process can also offer insight.

Phase 1: Incubation

Inspiration and invention usually follow vigorous *conscious* effort, accompanied by patient waiting and attention. This is the incubation phase. In the Cayce view, guidance on the path to new solutions for crises requires disciplined study and effort to prepare the way. What he offered was not blinding lightning, but steady sunlight in which plants properly tended could bloom and grow, sometimes with surprising speed.

Dreams offer useful illumination of the incubation process. For example, Cayce's readings showed two stockbrokers how to work with their dreams to gain clues and hunches on stocks. One of these men had the following amazing dream. He found himself standing before a lamppost at night. The light turned into all-encompassing illumination, and he saw every offering of the New York Stock Exchange, each with its quotes and trends, so that he could pick what he wanted. Using such dream clues, the man became a millionaire in his early thirties. But this did not happen without effort. The fruits of his dream came about only after months and months of hard, professional work on his part.

Disciplined, focused effort, in the Cayce view, prepares the way for the insightful energy of kundalini. Without this first stage, the psyche can simply be overwhelmed (as so many bad LSD experiences have demonstrated) or find answers to questions it has not asked, and which are therefore unintelligible.

One may properly observe that Cayce would have had to incubate a great deal to find himself giving aid by readings in so many fields! The answer in his counsel was that he had indeed prepared the way— not in one life, but in a series of lifetimes. By the same token, any of us may find the incubation proceeding slowly, under the pressure of crisis; yet now and then we might find an entirely new train of skills or concepts or values moving into consciousness, perhaps as the product of soul experiences during past lives. But most often the leap of inspiration starts with the plod of steady investment in the subject at hand, using all the conscious resources we have.

Dreams of the incubation process reflect the depth and steady unfolding of this stage. They often take us under the waters, as in the womb, or into the earth or caves. Relevant symbols of karma at work may include the ancient, the intricate, or the mythological. Dreams of the incubation process as such may naturally include pregnancy; or the courtship, foreplay, and intercourse that lead to conception. But they may also show creatures who run ahead of us, knowing where it is important to go—like Dorothy's dog, Toto, in *The Wizard of Oz*. Snakes and birds in dreams suggest our native wisdom is being awakened and focused; elephants bring their own reminders of long-term memory. Fruit and grain, trees and flowers evoke natural sprouting cycles, as do the seasons, and even the lifespans of stars and comets.

Phase 2: Startle

Poets and inventors alike know this stage. It is as delightful as it is awesome in its promise. The key is surmise: something good may happen to fit our pressing need. The term "startle" comes from the fact that the helpful outcome we suddenly glimpse or feel as possible is not necessarily what we expected. A new medicine or treatment direction may pop into mind; a friend who could get us a job may write us out of the blue; a constructive way to heal a rift may jump out of a dream.

A "click" of assurance marks this phase. Often people suck in their breath when it hits; the eyes widen, a tiny shiver moves through the flesh. When the stakes are very high, involving others as well as oneself, imagery may come dancing into awareness—not only of a remarkable outcome, but of old concepts seen with new eyes. In the Bible, for example, Mary speaks what has become known as the Magnificat when she is pregnant. Her soul guesses that the high will be low and the lowly high, when her star-marked child is born. Often we watched this phase operate when people sat listening to a Cayce reading, tears running down their faces, as though they had always known there must be a way for guidance to come quietly as from on high, but never thought they would see it.

Cayce suggests that the energy of this phase, as of the whole sequence, is of the divine. The first moments or intuitions are the movement of our own resources, given to us as potential cocreators, as they reach up to kiss the promise that we have correctly guessed, no matter how much trying effort may follow.

Dreams of this phase offer hints of the beginning of potent connections. We may participate in a bold feat, find a surprising lover, steer a difficult ship, ride a spirited horse, set out on a far journey. Images are often brief, because this is only the beginning. But they may be happily adventurous, as when they show a new wing on a building, or a new child or frolicking pet, or disclose a soaring peak through breaking clouds. A song or a shaft of light may signal that the impossible is now going to be possible. So may the presence of a beloved spiritual figure, or a welcome and inventive face from out of the past that is momentarily so vivid we could touch it.

The task of consciousness here is not to doubt, but to wait in trust for the next development. Premature announcement may tangle up the ego, or suggest the wrong course, because it is what we *think* we want. Yet when others must be mobilized for taxing work—for rescue of the captive or oppressed, for joint reception of healing, or for performing or building—it may be necessary to sing or speak or pray aloud during this phase. We need to be careful not to claim too much, but only to insist, with gratitude, on the reality of the gift that is promised and coming—somehow.

Phase 3: Lift

The next phase offers a lift in spirits, and a chance to collect our resources. It may directly follow the other phase, or come hours or days later; but there always emerges a welcome potency that engages the weary body as well as the baffled mind. We find ourselves ready to take on what comes, even failure, in a process of cocreating that feels worthwhile in itself. It may involve emotions of joy or awe or wonder, but it is not just enthusiasm (except in the primal sense of being en-Godded). No ecstasy is required, but rather a sense of steady blowing of the wind of the Spirit. We know deep down that serious business is afoot and a solution is coming.

During the lift new ideas begin to occur to us: where to advertise, whom to consult, where to get needed funds, what medication or bodywork will help, when to pray more steadily. The psyche is getting ready to rain its blessings, and we need to get our buckets out. People who came to see Cayce for a life-rescuing reading often reported this surging sense of lift, as real as the ocean bearing a craft across shoals, which accompanied them on their voyage to his presence.

Dreams reflect the unintoxicated but felicitous lift in their own ways: a riverbed starts to fill, rain falls on prairie grasses too long parched, the sun comes up. Partners meet for lovemaking, deeply enjoying each other's presence. Plants push up in the earth, animals come to a pool, unseen presences move across the background of a scene with their blessing, children dance, and prayers are spoken in worship with quiet authority. One way or another, the dream materials weave an assurance of potency and possibility and connection, even when all in waking life has seemed bleak and despairing.

Many find the lift phase so exciting that they fritter it away in chatter, particularly when it emerges in a group setting. Some make pomp out of something that should be simple, and offer portentous observations. But the disciplined mind, pledged to cocreating, only answers "Yes" as it gathers up the first manna, confident there will be more tomorrow morning, and gazes into the sky with thanks. Sometimes the lift itself is enough. Once we are popped out of our blues, we can remember an old solution that may work now, or guess correctly whom we should phone. If the needed solution is at hand, then it is appropriate to feast on it and share it. Otherwise, the process moves on.

Phase 4: Focus

During the focus phase, the energy seems to turn inward, asking, "Do you really want this? Can you afford the cost?" Moses wavers at the burning bush and asks for his brother. Jesus, starting his ministry, asks John to bury him in Jordan's water, and then flees to the wilderness to wrestle with the meaning of what is aroused in him, and how it might go astray. When the new solution threatens to call for more resources than we are sure we have, life gives us this merciful pause for focus. It is a time in which we can assess our purposes, our resolve, our companions, and our resources. We may say, "Not now," if that response is the best we know. Then the kundalini cycle of inspiration and fresh solutions will stop, offering only such blessings as it has already called forth. But if we feel the call to go further—forgive a marital partner, propose a new business direction, take a stand for funding a school of the handicapped—then this is the time to pledge all and risk all; not in dramatic poses, but in serious cocreating with our fellows and the One who sets us all moving.

When the focus phase begins, we need to realize that our own evil, pettiness, laziness, or willfulness can be laid bare for all to see, even while we are doing something that seems the best we know. The calls is always to *be*, not just to understand or enact. Like Arthur, we must pull our sword from our own rock. We must turn over rage at others to courage and humor. Lying must yield to positive inventiveness. We must embrace the wounded as well as the comely.

Whatever our darkness, it is likely to carry seeds of light. The dreams of this phase are not necessarily cheery, but grave—for the matters at hand are of death and rebirth, for ourselves and perhaps for others. Still, the promise is hidden in the challenge. A loved parent or teacher may be in the dream, as may a transcendent figure of our faith, or one who reminds us of that faith. We may be taken back in dreams to other streams we have crossed, schools we have entered, highways we have driven, cars we have owned, houses we have inhabited, as the unconscious counts our beads of blessings and strengthens us in the night.

More than before, we must engage our consciousness and will. This is decision time, not fantasy time. We have to count the cost, or our next state may be worse than the last. Who will help? What stockpiles can we draw upon? Where is the goodwill we need? Who are we to try to turn a death into a life-giving cause? Can we hold on, through bad times and good? Have we grown enough to grapple with circumstance on the one hand and our own demons on the other?

Phase 5: On

If we confidently answer "yes" to the mounting flow of inspiration and energy, then what follows can be astonishing. All that we are and have known begins to flow into awareness to help us. Long-forgotten skills return, as we type or cook or organize or do accounting with dispatch. We remember book titles and reference sources. We suddenly recall people with talents or funds who might help. All things seem to work together for good, often better than we might have hoped. Or we find we can take the bumps and betrayals and keep right on.

In Cayce's view, psychic happenings are especially prominent at this stage of inspiration or guidance. We somehow know who is on the phone, what is in the mail, how to handle a heartbroken teenager, where we mislaid a document. We can drive a car in fast traffic or ski with elegance, because our whole being is invested with energy and direction. In facing illness, we know when to order people out and pray, or when to invite people in and pray the prayer of hugs.

Cayce's perspective also suggests that good karma from past lives comes to us at this stage—we recall how to speak in public, forgive an old enemy, perform a song or rite. We can figure things out, assign resources, take charge, in ways that only recently would have seemed unlikely or impossible. Harmony and energy and insight bless us. But temptation to parade our feats comes with their performance, and we may tumble into hubris as fast as Moses did in battle, or as readily as King David took Bathsheba to bed. We feel invincible, not realizing that it is the spirit in us, and the Spirit ever more with us, which is invincible—not our limited heads and hearts.

Dreams during the on phase tell us that we are standing in the true stream of what Cayce called the Creative Forces. We dream of flowers that cover the hillside with abundant promise; light glistens off the lowliest office desk as though it were an altar; meals are served to a table foursquare or even a Round Table; we leap into the air or fly; classes are held for us and problems explained so well that we waken with lists in our heads, or drawings that depict the play of forces around us. The veil of death may part for a greeting of someone loved, or we may see the needs of someone far away yet dear to us. Even healing may visit us as we sleep, so that we awaken clear-eyed and strong after debilitating illness. When the life force crests at this phase, dreams not only carry information, they actually affect us.

The conscious mind has every right to use the skills, energy, and understanding conferred during this period, providing it is keeping its promises as to who will be given the benefits, and is willing for anonymity. Suffering and loss may follow later, but this is the time to marshal all that is good and helpful. If, by the grace of what has been awakened, our problem is now solved and crisis met or transformed, then we need go no further. We can end the flow with moments of unfeigned gratitude. But if the dark wall remains, we must choose to go on, though we know not what may follow.

Phase 6: Stumbling

Just when we think we might turn out to be invincible, or that the gods are carrying us in their hands, problems arise. The sources are not surprising. Heavy demands are being made on the psyche. Old wounds open up, in us and in others. One archetype activated awakens another, as love needs its twin, wisdom, to keep from overwhelming the beloved; wisdom needs love to keep from saying too much too fast about what it sees. When great pressures have come to bear, the earth of our lives must shift under our feet; and the upset may be considerable.

Typically, in this phase, we exhaust the money, somebody pulls out of the deal, or we think we are falling in love with a coworker when it is actually our guardian angel that has come so close. The disease recurs; the angry words fly again; the plans don't fit. We are dismayed. Have the gods turned against us? Are we now to be punished for old guilt and sins? From the Cayce perspective, the chakras are being invested with strong force, and their weaknesses show along with their strengths. In the same way, and using the same centers, karma that has been called up brings its wounds and fears and doubts, as well as its strengths (this will be discussed in chapter six). The knowledge that this phase is part of the process of inspiration and fresh beginnings can give us the courage and patience to hold on.

In this phase, we dream of destruction: houses tumbling off weak foundations, cars that need serious repair, famine or storms or earthquakes. The dream intent is not to drive us wild with dour portents, but to share with us the magnitude of the effort under way. Dreams of delivery of a child (or that other delivery, dying) are not uncommon. We dream we are warriors wearing over-large or rusted armor, which we must exchange for a lowly David's slingshot—still surprisingly effective. We must venture into swamps or floods to find a treasure, or try to find the light switch in the engulfing darkness. Often we must help someone else in order to help ourselves, which is as true in waking as in sleep. Carrying a stranger across a river, we may be carrying the Christ unknown. When we stumble on the path, the ones we have helped now help us.

In the stumbling phase, consciousness needs to exercise patience and trust. The very force of awakened archetypes makes them dangerous, like steeds that can be ridden yet can also trample. Time is required to tame the strong resources, without quenching their fire. We should consider the blows and barriers that now arise as messages of assurance that real, lasting business is being done, in us and around us. If the stages before this one have been real and rewarding, faith can tell us to go on. Only those willing to walk up to a tomb can discover that it is empty on Easter.

Phase 7: Overshadowing

If the course of inspiration, healing, or reconciliation must continue, what happens next can hardly be believed by those who have not experienced it. The on phase is miracle enough; as it pulls together knowledge and skills and memories in a dance of happy potency, it is as much psychic as it is attainment. But now we enter the realm where energy or spirit or love from beyond the natural kundalini cycle enters the circuit. All that is meant by God as Comforter now becomes so real that it briefly stops the breathing or brings tears. We suddenly know what to say when thought and words have run out; we understand when someone's anger masks fear; we grasp where the building should be placed or the curriculum revised or the revolution begun. All this is gift, to the wise soul. Few who experience it claim otherwise. We may lay hands upon the ill and have their flesh respond in welcome health, just as we may tame a rebellious animal or understand a balky machine.

We do not become gods, and we do not know everything. But we become godly: we know what we need, as character and potency meet and bow to each other. Blind Samson knew the strength of this stage as he pulled down the unworthy temple; but so have others, who endured death camps they could not tear down. Singers phrase their songs so well that they wound all listening hearts; and physicians know where to insert electrodes that have not been tried before. Astronauts stare at the blue earth and weep for its loveliness; others stare at the face of a homeless child and know it is epiphany. Mohammed smashes idols that have policed the deserts for eons, and millions will embrace him for it, because Allah replaces the idols with his indescribable Oneness. A mother trying to help her frightened and ill child suddenly knows what to apply to the fevered body, and how to croon a healing song from her own childhood.

To speak of these moments as psychic is to beggar them—as well call a sweeping sunset a fine street lamp. But the sheer joyous gift—

brief as it may be—of exactly what is needed for the darkest crisis, carries with it redoubled danger to the unsteady head. If we claim for ourselves what is lent us at this time, we suffer the fate of Moses, who was not allowed to go with his people across Jordan; for the Presence does not often revisit those who play games with it. To be sure, we may see that what transpires is in some way related to all we have studied and practiced and analyzed, so that it is not an alien invasion. Our own archetypes are used, not those of another. But the deployment is not our attainment, for here the Ultimate bends low, and the hushed recipient murmurs "Father" or "Adonai" or whatever aspiration and habit brings to the tongue.

Often, in this phase, the flesh trembles involuntarily. Fortunately this kind of visitation rarely lasts long, extending for a few timeless moments or perhaps as long as an hour and a half. The clean love shoots through us so freely that we marvel we can sustain it, while all of nature looks scrubbed and shiny. Sometimes, in trance, Cayce's quiet voice went beyond its usual regular speech to inspired images and tones, carried along by compassion that drew sudden wisdom in its wake. Not a few wept softly as they listened to directions for saving a dying infant or a troubled marriage or a foundering cause. The overshadowing is just as real today as it was in ancient times, for those who will work for it and wait upon it—not just for themselves, but also for others.

Dreams of this phase may bring symbols remembered for years. A great cathedral on a plane, a single shaft of color, a melody never heard again, a silence that even angels would honor, a great old tree grown up through a roof, a rock that cannot be moved—all of these tell of the transcendent visiting the utterly familiar. Images come that are too powerful for words; the very spin of the soul is disclosed in its cosmic reach, the Godhead made thinkable in dreams of purposeful force.

These dreams are not spiritual entertainment, but empowerment for specific tasks and specific needs. Dream contents tell us where we are to spend ourselves, because the hearts of others are heavy and minds dulled, or spirits lonely. The energy of this phase is so collected, so coherent, so purposeful, that those who experience it are not surprised that Jericho's walls could be shattered, just as can the hearts of those who torment or neglect the ragged poor today. This phase in dreams—just as in waking—illuminates the tenderness in the prostitute, the discipline of the thief, the extravagant longing of the addict, just as it shows us what is good and noble beneath the pretentious in ourselves and those we would help. The sun shines upon the just and unjust alike, as dreams remind us how great is the love that enfolds us all in our too-tight skins of separateness.

What we need from consciousness and the poised will for this phase is readiness to serve. We must bet all on the guidance and energy offered, and not mind those who do not understand. Too many words are traps.

Phase 8: Release

The gifted English mystic, Walter Hilton, said of the blessed stillness and melted light that run through one's consciousness and body in the fullness of meditation: "Once having known it, one may not undesire it." So it is with overshadowing of any kind. But longing for its return does not mean trying to coerce it. Rather, we must respond with gratitude and confidence. We may call out our gratitude in words or signal it with gestures. Only the grateful heart is clean enough to be a chalice for another time. Ancient rites may help, whether of kneeling or happy dance, or blessing the neighbor with a hug or kiss. In olden times, the patriarchs put up a mound of stones, to mark that Yahweh met them in this place, so they would find it and be reminded when next they passed by, chasing their sheep or dodging marauders. Stones may look strange in a kitchen or a bedroom or a boardroom, or on the street or in a sanctuary. But plants will not, nor the crayoned drawings children give us, which try to capture the infinite in scraggly lines and bursting color.

Confidence will carry us on. After we have found our way up the long mountain of inspiration, all the way to the Most High, every other slope is just a hill. Crises may again hit us with tornado force, but we are confident that Something knows the way, and wants to show it to us. Martyrs facing lions in arenas or trapped in *gulags* are confident that their suffering is not pointless, having been graced by the glory that cannot be painted.

Over the couch where he gave readings, Cayce kept all sorts of photos pinned to the wall. Most of them were unposed, given him by friends he had helped. When he had to lie down into darkness each day to go into trance, he could glance at these untidy mementos and draw from them the courage he needed to keep on. In the release phase, we can each find such confidence from the countenances of those we know well in the daily round, understanding that in receiving the gifts of their personhood, we may receive sweaty angels unawares.

Dreams of the release phase deposit a golden silt in our veins. We waken in the morning to know that whatever must be done is doable, while the impossible takes only a bit longer. We can bury the dead, leave behind the old job, end the shallow relationship, carry the clumsy, caress the unlovely, because we understand that life is gift. In our dreams, we steer ships with ease, conduct orchestras, lead pilgrims, take charge of meetings. We are serene and buoyantly confident. The unconscious is determined to leave its mark, make its pile of stones in consciousness, and it seizes whatever is precious to us for the nighttime task.

The response of consciousness, graced by the full cycle of inspiration in time of crisis, is not simply to revel in its fortune, but to give thanks and move on. We have training to do, so that in crisis we may help ourselves and others with hope. To that training we turn now.

5

Getting Past Doubt, Finding New Solutions

THE PROMISE OF THE Cayce resource—that we each have a remarkable capacity for finding positive solutions to crises—reaches even farther than the phases of inspiration we have just considered. Cayce's readings stressed that his gift was not unique, or a fluke of nature, but instead exemplified a process open to everyone in varying measure. These readings, and Cayce's life, presented both psychic or intuitive perception and psychokinesis (what is often referred to as mind over matter) as natural processes at work in all of us.

HOW WE USE PSYCHIC ABILITY EVERY DAY

The Cayce readings tell us that we are using psychic ability all the time. We constantly solve problems or protect ourselves and loved ones with the aid of "hunches," psychic cues slipped into consciousness from the unconscious.

Recent research supports this thesis, as exemplified by the work of parapsychologist Rex Stanford and others on psi-mediated instrumental response (PMIR). In this process, people being challenged by one ESP task, which they know about, may also show surprising success on a concurrent ESP task, which is kept hidden from them. Similarly, research on telepathy in dreams, by Montague Ullman and

Stanley Krippner and others, shows that some subjects are highly effective at incorporating into their dreams elements of randomly chosen images "sent" telepathically by researchers. This research supports the Cayce thesis that psi (a generic name for psychic capacities) is often at work in dreams. Cayce's readings even argue that every important development in our lives is previewed in dreams—whether as an implication of current trends, or as direct psychic inspection, or both.

Other research suggests comparable sensitivity at work in non-dream states. Widely repeated remote viewing research, in which ordinary people try to "see" and draw what a distant experimenter is seeing and "sending," again suggests that all of us may have inherent psychic ability, and may participate directly in some version of what Cayce did in his readings.

If we are all more psychic than we realize, then the prospect of finding new solutions to crises takes on added adventure. The following story from the ranks of those exploring Cayce-suggested methods of dream study illuminates this point.

An individual in Australia suffered for several years from debilitating weakness and sensory impairment. Unable to find the reason with expert medical aid, he saw in a dream a precise case number from the Cayce files of readings, far off in Virginia. His interest piqued, he sent for the transcript. The case turned out to be one of mercury poisoning, and the symptoms were identical to his. With this information, the Australian was able to discover exactly where and how he had been similarly poisoned by mercury, and to receive appropriate treament that produced a complete cure. Such experiences among those not known professionally as "psychic" serve to heighten attention to the Cayce claim that all of us have astonishing resources.

HOW PAST LIVES CAN HELP US SOLVE TODAY'S PROBLEMS

Part of the problem-solving promise offered in the Cayce readings is more difficult to establish by today's research methods: that crises also can spring loose an inheritance of talents and seasoned know-how, or systematic understanding and inventiveness, from one or more prior lives. If this claim should prove durable under continued investigation (along lines pioneered by Ian Stevenson, M.D., and his associates at the University of Virginia Medical School), then we have even more telling assets for recreating our circumstances and personhood when loss or blind misfortune visit us.

Using dreams, guided reveries, and projective tests, we have been helping individuals for decades (in our counseling and psychotherapy, as well as in our business consulting) to recover what seem to be past-life resources or to disengage past-life panics. These hundreds of cases are only suggestive, and oftentimes capable of interpretation as the awakening of helpful archetypes rather than as specific prior-life memories; but they provide evidence that many or most of us have more latent resources than we guess for dealing with crises of loving, laboring, spirituality, and selfhood.

For example, a young mother who was overly attached to her parents found a helpful dream clue (supported by other interests and attractions) that she was influenced by a prior Chinese incarnation in which reverence for ancestors was central. She was then able to sort out what was useful and harmful in her present orientation. A social worker given to emotional binges found in his lifelong attraction to Hinduism clues to the love of orgiastic Shakti energies, and made better progress in taming his excesses. A young woman who had dropped out of college, mistrusting her intellectual capacities, took a trip to Greece. There she found reinforcing assurance of her orderly mind, cultivated long ago in a life in ancient Greece. She proved it with straight As when she went back to school—not forgetting to take courses in Greek classics!

Looking for answers in past lives, in our clinical experience, requires picking one's way through a prickly thicket of alternative explanations. But for many, the effort has proved exciting when suffering, hardship, failure, or crisis has demanded radical approaches.

TAMING DOUBT

When our spirits sag, doubt creeps in to cloud the mind and keep us from knowing where to turn. Two kinds of doubt are particularly crippling: doubt of ourselves, and doubt of God.

Two Kinds of Doubt

When we hear of people like Albert Schweitzer, who are able to turn distress into delivery, we are all tempted to say, "I could never do that!" Professionals who work intensively with a range of sufferers are often struck by the pervasiveness of such self-doubt. Perhaps its seeds can be found in faulty parenting, which has saddled the individual with hopeless standards, or doubt of reward for effort. Such parents may have undercut the individual with lack of primal celebration and cherishing, or misled the person into indulgence and self-pity. Whether such seeds are met by predisposition from past lives may fairly be left open to further investigation. What matters here is the widespread tendency to say that others may be able to find buckets and bail themselves out, but we are not likely to do so.

We each have ways of backing off from heavy demands. Some people are perfectionists, who do not want to start without guaranteed results; others are fantasizers, who like to believe that everything will work out by itself; still others are just generally soured on the human condition by unhappy relationships and projects. We doubt not only our own competence and endowments, but more deeply doubt our self-worth. Sometimes that doubt is a cry for rescue; we so magnify our despair that we think the heavens will break in compassion. Sometimes the doubt is a cry for let-up in responsibility, when we have already strained ourselves for years to give what we think others require from us. Sometimes the doubt is well founded—when we survey the wreckage around us from a jail cell, a broken marriage, an alcohol or drug addiction, or an illness brought on by poor self-care. Deeper yet, we may be participating in a common human anxiety of loneliness in the universe. We cannot estimate the weight of our failures nor the possibility of tender forgiveness and fresh starts, from what seems impersonal nature, arbitrary fate, or manipulative society.

Sometimes we doubt the existence or compassion of God. When we feel trapped, and every empty chair reminds us of someone close who has just died, or every auto accident speaks of a smashed relationship with a lover, or every stock decline signals the decline in our hopes for a better education or job, we may well wonder where God is. If there is a God, then he/she is off doing something else, or cannot get hold of events, or tends only to those more devout than we.

As we shall see, the Cayce resource offers some fresh views about the relationship between what seems to be arbitrary suffering and the will and way of the divine. As a first step, it offers two ways to begin dealing with both kinds of doubts. One is to enlarge prayer with meditation. The other is to find love by giving it, even in a world that may seem bent on self-destruction, following ends that are often far from noble.

Prayer

Counselors sometimes hear relatives asking physicians about a patient: "What can we do?" If the answer is, "Pray," then the alarmed response follows, "Is it that bad?" The presumption is that prayer is only appropriate when all else fails. Yet we would not phone our dearest friends only in emergencies and expect to have the friendships mean much.

Lively prayer has a better analogue in the doings of lovers, who find when they are separated that no day's events are complete and meaningful until they are shared by phone or letter or reunion with the beloved. Life seems only partially real until the companion is engaged in it. Precisely the same perspective fits the challenge of having the divine as companion in prayer. A different perspective comes from those who live near a vast natural resource—the mountains and giant trees of the Pacific Northwest, the shores of the vast Atlantic, the sweeping plains of the Midwest. Residents of such settings always know, as their dreams suggest, just where the larger reality lies. They can direct strangers by this orientation, and keep their own perspective as well.

It is only a step from such beloved geography to keeping one's bearings by the Eternal, in prayer. Great cities have their own symbolism, too, and the people we counsel often dream plots that utilize the regions and neighborhoods of cities. But cities are culture, and the most potent dreams link them with rivers or ports that come from beyond culture; the combination of human creation and transhuman creation stirred the writer of Psalm 46 to say, "God is in the midst of her; she shall not be moved"; just as Ishmael, in opening Herman Melville's *Moby Dick*, marvels at how urban humans are ever drawn to water.

The Cayce approach to prayer is not to offer pleas for benefits, preceded by dutiful appreciation and polite contrition. Rather, it is learning to be *in* prayer, to walk in its light as one might stride through shafts of sunlight in a forest. First comes intent—the cry of the heart for relationship, not for a shopping list of wants. From the visionary viewpoint of Cayce's readings, prayer belongs in the same category as medical care. Healing of cells and organs and limbs requires tuning up, or calling forth, the final vibrations of atoms, until they sing again the song of productive health, wholeness ready to be given away.

Cayce's readings often suggested an approach to a prayer-infused life with a phrase that hearers were encouraged to put in their own words: "Lord, let me be a channel of blessings to others." The imagery of flow in channels is no accident: Cayce's concept of prayer is of streams of living energies, not simply periodic dialogues with the divine. The blessing is classically a longing for the well-being of another, or a cry of thanksgiving, rather than a calculated petition for rewards. So it was the fitting emblem for prayer that Cayce's readings used, to start others afresh on the journey of communing with the divine.

Once we grasp the concept of flow and put it to work in prayer, then it is time to speak of change and direction. In Cayce's readings, and in his life, the next element of prayer was often, "Not my will but Thine be done." His intent was not to disparage individual effort; for in this view each soul is unspeakably precious to the divine who called it forth at the beginning. According to the Cayce readings, a soul that does not use its own will, with its discriminating mind and inventive spirit, is a soul hardly alive. His intent was rather encouragement to make the discovery (which Cayce's readings warned was so often difficult for humans) that putting one's deep trust in God does not take away one's freedom and uniqueness, but only enhances it. Few who have fallen deeply in love, or grown there, would report that trusting another—even to the point of becoming crucially vulnerable—serves to make one's life more shallow, and make one's personhood shrink, even though blows and disappointments may follow. So it is with the relationship that prayer expresses: longing and delight and trust are at the heart of it.

As we step ever deeper into the mystery of communing with the One in prayer, our sense of gratitude and thanksgiving grows. Just as lovers are prompted to present each other with gifts and surprises, God becoming more real is God to be celebrated, enjoyed, sung about, and danced about. Yet this delight brings with it awe at the glory one glimpses or seems momentarily to touch, so that the journey of prayer becomes as freely contrition as celebration. Lovers who hurt each other, or neglect each other, want to stop it and try to do so. So the soul that leaps up into God's light finds the shadows of unworthiness more real, not less; it hungers often for righteousness and a fresh start.

Cayce's counsel was repeatedly to seek God's forgiveness—not in abasement, to please an arbitrary ruler; but in that earnest turning around, which in human terms would be an embrace, sometimes in tears. Again the counsel was to find the process by doing it with one's fellows, whether lovers or those who hurt us (and who hurts us more than lovers and others we truly cherish?): "Forgive as ye would be forgiven."

Then the flow of prayer might seek guidance, healing, or alleviation of broken dreams and bitter loss. Who would not bring these to a lover? But trying to become a lover just to get favors cheapens the relationship. Petition, in this view, is the outgrowth of a daily relationship, not the first basis for that relationship. Yet the Cayce readings do not suggest that God is indifferent to the cries of those who forget the divine. As truly as parents wait unforgetting upon their errant children, the One is never far away from the call of a penitent heart seeking to do justly and love mercy. Cayce's call to nurture a relationship as the heart of prayer does not mean one cannot begin it at any time in the shattering moments of crisis. If strangers help each other crawl out of wrecked planes, full of unsuspected compassion and helpfulness, would not God do as much and more for a smashed life?

Cayce's biography shows what his readings warmly suggested: prayer blossoms best in the garden of committed fellowship. The prayer of one may, in a flash of ESP and more, unlock the heavy spirit of another. Prayer seems especially powerful when people come together for the study and rites that make up corporate worship, family prayers, office sharing, and small-group seeking. To miss the larger setting of prayer in gathered life of the like-minded, set in the round of the church year or other religious cycles, would be having to reinvent the wheel. It would be forever courting and never marrying and having children, nor building a better town and a better world for these lives to sprout in.

Meditation

All of these reflections on prayer, so deep in Cayce's readings as in his life, are familiar in the West. Cayce's readings also added a less familiar element: meditation.

Cayce's counsel advises each of us to give periodic attention to our dreams, as part of wholesome and productive human existence. It invites all to consider psychic experience as part of the human birthright. Likewise, Cayce's counsel recommends meditation for everyone, not just for saints and ascetics and religious functionaries.

In the view of these readings, meditation is a natural complement to prayer, as a kind of listening to God that belongs with speaking to God. Using the metaphor of flow, the readings often described meditation as allowing certain "coded energies" to arise and do their work in one's being (along kundalini channels), in consort with the prayer that gives direction and commitment to that being. In prayer, as in much of worship, we fill the mind with the radiance and goodness of the divine. In meditation, we empty consciousness, so that a deeper flow might take place.

Conception is one of the more colorful images for meditation used in the Cayce readings. In the silence that completes spoken or visualized prayer, seeds of new life can sprout and grow to maturity. But it is crucial that these be good seeds: for the effect of sustained and regular meditating is to lift up into the very structure of the psyche, and even of the flesh, that which is "on the mind" and "in the heart." Here the formulation and celebration of chosen ideals—especially the central ideals of godliness—can be seen in their crucial role, around which all others could best rotate, as planets around the sun.

To make sure that the energies of meditation go in this direction, rather than following errant cravings or schemes in the deeper recesses of the mind, Cayce counseled that prayer and study accompany meditation, and then find their echo in a guiding phrase, affirmation, or mantra, which sums up the best aspirations and the longed-for relationship. This is not to be used mechanically, but as a focal point that can be held very gently. The intent is not to fill the mind again, with words or even symbols (ever the temptation when consciousness steps aside); but only with wordless Reality, which might be suggested by light or vibration or some other pattern beyond words. (Ultimately meditation is love, coming to life in the flesh and the psyche. But even this reality so tempts the mind to imagery that Cayce's readings often fell back upon the generic term "Creative Forces.")

What effect does meditation have on primal doubt? When it is linked to total companionship with God, and not undertaken simply as spiritual hygiene or conjuring, it awakens the same vital energies and sense of worth that doubt corrodes. One may not be able to name when it happens, or how, but the result of meditating is often new personal confidence and joy of living. Those who practice it will not readily give it up—even though the effort sometimes falters, as with any discipline. In the same way, meditation works to tame the doubt of God's loving presence and concern, without in itself answering all the questions of the restless mind. It makes certain hypotheses more believable, in its own way, just as a gentle kiss between lovers speaks of a mutual trust that will bear the later strains of marriage and rearing a family.

The Cayce readings do not offer meditation as a panacea, though some have seen it that way, in their hunger to find a replacement for old rituals that have lost their meaning. Nor is it presented as an act complete in itself. Meditation cries out for action, sharing, creating, just as a newly tuned instrument might tremble with the sound of another playing nearby. In the theory of kundalini that undergirded Cayce's serious theorizing about meditation, the flow is incomplete until the vital forces raised in the stillness are expressed in cradling a child, planting a crop, forming a worthwhile argument, making a friend of an antagonist. Unless spent in service, this attunement is not only fruitless, but ultimately dangerous. For faithful meditation awakens no less than the life force itself, however named; and the only way to handle it is to move it on in some wisely chosen direction. "We only keep what we give away," Cayce counseled in many a reading. Otherwise, as not a few New Age seekers have discovered, as have mystics of stature before them, the same life-renewing energy strikes inward to produce restlessness, irritability, and ultimately even illness. The One sought in silence may not be sought for self-glorification, for the only glory that lasts is headed for sharing.

FINDING CREATIVITY BY GIVING IT: EIGHT STEPS TO CONQUERING DOUBT

In our confusing times, it is easy to feel powerless in the face of personal crises. Institutions—business, government, sports, or media—seem huge and impersonal. Nuclear winter seems inevitable. AIDS is becoming increasingly prevalent. Terrorists kill innocent victims. Advertising, pornography, and violence in entertainment portray people as things. Crime and grafitti disfigure our neighborhoods. Drug pushers hover around high school proms. Heads of state taunt each other like bullies, while their deadly hardware depletes everyone's supply of eatables and wearables. Why should we not doubt both our own power and God's? What can we do to dissolve this feeling of impotence?

Cayce's readings and his life suggest eight different ways in which we can begin to tame the dragons of doubt and helplessness. These eight ways can teach us our real nature and help us cocreate with the divine. Together, they constitute the practice of helping, which matches the practice of prayer and meditation, when we ask with the full Cayce resource how to join attunement and service to create richer lives. These steps may seem unusual at first, and they all require effort. But our experience is that most adults can do all eight, and find them welcome adventures.

1. Learn About One Other Culture

Goethe once wrote that the person who knows one language knows none. We cannot truly claim the treasures of our own heritage until we have some means to compare them with others. When we learn about another culture, we learn about humanity.

The challenge in step 1 is to pick one people who are not our own native folk and tongue, and become an authority and resource for others on these people. We need not be scholars. The idea is not to impress the learned, but to help the impressionable learn—to aid those who really want to know. In the process, we will also learn. Having another culture means having another perspective. Having another culture so close that we can sing its songs, dance its dances, smell its demons, hope its dreams means that we can see with new eyes our own family life, political action, religious transformation, roles of men and women, racial justice, or whatever else comes our way for decision and action.

This task is not out of reach of anyone who will choose to become a candle of light in a dark time. You might buy books about the chosen country and people, get tapes of their music, collect a bit of their art, follow their current events in the news. You might invite home exchange students from that country, and travel to their land when you can afford it (these days it is surprising how quickly that opportunity can come around, when you seek it). Whether you travel or not, you might still help send a young person there, complete with guidebooks and some language tapes you have supplied, so that another life besides yours will see all of culture and history more richly, ever after.

Once you have established your knowledge, you need to get the word out in your community that you are a resource. Make it known that you have books and articles on these people that students can use as a resource for term papers and school reports. If you can make or collect slides and show them, sharing from your heart, that is better still; and talks for community groups are within the reach even of the shy. You might consult with bookstores and libraries on what to carry, and keep tour folders for traveling relatives and friends.

If you can learn something of the language of your chosen people, do—for with it comes the inner archetypes of a people, with all their ambiguity. Serving abroad with the Peace Corps or a religious agency, or going on academic sabbaticals, is possible right into your senior years. Some corporations, such as IBM, grant sabbaticals with partial pay for employees who want to spend a period in overseas service. But whether your participation in the pilgrimage of another people is small or large, it needs to be coupled with prayer for them and their leaders. (Cayce's sister told the authors how, as a boy, he named specific overseas mission concerns when it was his turn to offer table grace in their farm family.)

You may choose to learn about an ancient culture, knowing that history also has its treasures. Cayce's entire life was marked by the journey with one other culture: the biblical Israelites. Everything he touched that mattered to him shone with comparisons from this double vision. To be sure, choosing this people led him to the other cultures by which the Israelites were deeply affected for better and worse: Egypt, Assyria, Persia, Greece, Rome.

If we choose wisely the people and the land for our specialization, there is every reason, from the Cayce perspective, to expect that we will obtain an unexpected treasure: the best of one or more of our own past lives. It will be awakened by what we take on now, and screened to draw forth the treasures without the regrets, by our purpose of building a better world today. Some people who are interested in reincarnation suspect that one reason for the widespread ritual of learning a foreign language in school, even though it is little used in later years, is the gift it brings of past-life currents within the individual who seeks to find a people, not just a vocabulary and grammar. Nor is it beyond reason to suspect that some of us (if reincarnation is factual) may also prepare for a lifetime elsewhere by becoming a resource now, and arriving there later with a running start. Whatever the long-range outcome of choosing to study a certain people, the short-range result is likely to be taming of doubts—of ourselves and of the hand of God in human affairs. It can all begin with a couple of books on the coffee table.

2. Become a Helper on One Social Problem

Becoming a helper on a social problem can be profoundly rewarding, as we discovered during four years of living intimately within the grace and pain of racial and cultural struggles in Chicago's black and Japanese neighborhoods. You don't actually have to move to enter fully into this venture beyond doubt; indeed, live-in action is too often limited to drastic needs. The goal, as in step 1, is to become an active community resource. It is important to focus on *one* social problem so that you do not get overwhelmed by social need and social conflicts.

For example, you might choose homelessness, hunger, a particular endangered species, child abuse, drug abuse, nutrition, Native American rights, AIDS, housing, breast cancer, access for the handicapped, migrant workers, feminist roles, nuclear freeze, couples in ministry, adolescent runaways, or problems of the elderly. We have helped individuals weakened by crises to take on each of these and more, one per person or one per couple. Whether to choose the area of one's own great pain is not easy to decide. Often, as AA has shown, deep healing is the result of the effort to help others who have a similar problem. But sometimes an entirely new focus is refreshing, and less fraught with initial anxiety.

You can begin to become a resource on a specific social problem in your own community by collecting books, articles, tapes, and booklets, then lending them out. Religious groups often have entire packets of materials from several sources, available for you to collect at low cost. Students need your resources for reports; churches and synagogues and community organizations need them for programs. The best resources not only describe a problem, but tell who is finding solutions and how. Marilyn Ferguson's *The Aquarian Conspiracy* has inspired many to find out what others are doing in important areas of social distress and worthwhile change.

It is essential to build a file of model programs to visit, whether you get to go there or not (often you will find a way to visit, discovering that researchers or social workers or other laborers on location welcome your truly informed interest). Invite specialists in your community to visit you for coffee or a meal, and welcome others who are interested. You may even want to help develop an existing or new network, as Ferguson so well describes. Or you may want to pitch in and help one day a week at a crisis center or helping effort that deals with your chosen concern.

It is not necessary to turn your commitment into a crusade. But discovering that people of goodwill are hard at work building a new world, and giving them a hand, tames doubt. It is not unlikely that you may want to contribute money or extra copies of resources that come your way to programs you care about. Business executives are often willing to go out of their way to hire dispossessed farmers, convicts looking for a new beginning, the handicapped, the elderly, or some other category of individuals for whom a helping hand can be a lifesaver.

One of the privileges for any of us as truly informed people can be to help facilitate such connections. Some who read of this challenge may think they have found the path by keeping up with the news. But hearing and doing are different processes, and specializing gets us beyond dabbling in a little good here and a little there. So does regular prayer for specific leaders and movements in the social concern we take on. Such prayer, if it is matched by actions, quickly shifts from duty to privilege.

Cayce made himself a special resource in two avenues: the one the kind of health care that today is called holistic medicine, and the other the problems of convicts and prisons. He kept himself informed (chiefly by conversations, but also by reading articles and news reports) on then-alternative treatment modalities such as osteopathy and hydrotherapy and prayer healing, and he kept a file of physicians and researchers ready to help others with like interests. He wrote to responsive leaders in these fields, and went to visit clinics; he asked for reports on sufferers he referred to medical centers, and regularly gave readings without charge to physicians.

Lifting the burden from sufferers, especially those deemed incurable, was not just the business of his readings; it was a central commitment for himself and his household. Together they helped inventors build new treatment devices in the basement of the Cayce home. Table grace in this family, like the prayers that preceded his trances, were not ritual mumbling, but kept the candle of concern lit before the Most High, for the medical needs of those whom they took on.

When he was only twenty-one and a bookstore clerk in Louisville, before he had given any readings, Cayce took on the problems of convicts and prisons. All his life, wherever he lived, he went regularly (often weekly) to visit those in jail or prison. He brought them reading materials, shared the Bible, taught them to read or to pray, or helped them plan new occupations and new associations. He involved his family, a few of whom kept up the practice long after his death, and he set a pattern that some A.R.E. members have followed for years, all around the country. Prisoners who wanted his friendship and aid after they served their sentences got it freely—including readings given without charge, and assistance in finding jobs and housing. Often he kept the churches where he taught busy meeting such needs. As a result, he drew courage for his own peculiar vocation. But he drew an even deeper conviction, which all who knew him well encountered: that God would forgive any contrite heart, and always had a plan to help an individual begin afresh, even in circumstances where freedom and hope seemed lost.

3. Help to Start One Self-Help Program

Delight and potency erase doubt when we join with others to start and develop something truly needed. The project may not engage serious social problems at all, but just provide a constructive boost to better living. You might open a health-food store or restaurant; start a new choral group or orchestra; open a child-care center; start a library and bookstore in a church or synagogue; start a food or book co-op; and even start a hospice, a burial society, or an alternative school.

What matters here is not just newness, but getting baptized in all the steps of creating a piece of a better world, so that you can do more and different things later, and share with others the steps traversed. Keeping a journal of meetings and budgets and pitfalls can be fun, and invaluable to others, though many adventurers get too busy to do it. Looking for facilities, finding volunteers, scraping up funds, trying to schedule events, traveling together to see how others have done it, hiring staff and developing policies and manuals, wrestling with where to allocate too few dollars—all of these make us true cocreators, not just chanters of the Creator's praises.

It is tempting to get into this life-giving process by fashioning a vehicle funded by government, whether local or national; but most of those who have done it recommend starting with private funding or resources first. Old attitudes of dependency on authorities, or hostility to them, do not surface as quickly among the cobuilders. When we are serious about our chosen projects, we will start or end the day with an explicit prayer of blessing for them, asking for God's guidance and gift of presence in the ordinary. And we will eat meals with blessings that bear the others in mind who seek to build where nothing stood before.

Just doing your project can boost spirits. But going on to show others how to do it, and trying the process in new settings, keeps you alive and stretching, and sure that you are not helpless in an often-impersonal society. In time, you may risk larger entities—a new political or social action group, a new hospital or health center, a magazine, a special museum, an innovative business, a new design for developing a town or city. Too often in our affluent suburbs we simply "want the best" for ourselves and our children, and try to buy excellence from elsewhere, whether athletic coaches, rock groups, or medical specialists. But just consuming the culture without ever renewing it is parasitical, and betrays a hidden part of the best: what we can do together when we make up our minds and hearts, starting right where we are.

Cayce bet himself and his assets on building a hospital with his friends. The process was the toughest single challenge of his life, because everyone who touched the enterprise grew, though not without pain. Many helped because they were fascinated with his gift, and wanted their own benefits of business guidance or fame or learning; but some did it in the lovely and fierce joy of being cocreators for the worthwhile. He got the hospital, and a university besides. When he lost them both, he found he still had something alive in him and his closest associates that would not go away. The courage and vision he drew from his efforts kept him training others for years afterwards, confident that in time they would build even better structures and recruit new laborers, ready to discover their own resources, even when half-blinded by personal crises—as indeed they have done.

4. Cooperate with the Earth and Its Creatures

One of the more daunting assertions in Cayce's readings is the insistence that everyone should aim for a life-round with immediate access to the soil—for growing food and rearing creatures, as well as creating gardens and trees. Obviously, to wean an entire civilization away from huge cities is a tall order. But initial efforts can be made toward new kinds of communities, such as Paolo Soleri's Arcosanti in Arizona, or the kibbutzim of Israel, or the communes of China. America had its Civilian Conservation Corps in Depression days, where the young served and renewed the land rather than drilling in the military.

The challenge of step 4 is to begin the engagement oneself—somehow, somewhere. A beginning is always possible, even if you start by planting flowers in a crowded apartment building; making a shared garden in a vacant lot; or creating a retreat center or church camp where individuals and groups may take their turns truly engaging nature's work (not just patronizing it). The magazine of creation spirituality, *Creation*, bursts with suggestions and reports in each beautifully illustrated and often poetic issue, where the process of engaging nature is stretched beyond the earth as soil to engaging the earthy in cooking, sexuality, and finally global peacemaking. What is needed is a beginning, a regular engagement of that which grows from its own seeds or kind. Today, when armaments and shopping complexes overwhelm us, it is easier to watch TV shows on Africa's natural wonders than to care for our own plants and pets, or grow something that we and our neighbors need to eat. We need to build our arks with Noah, going back to the creatures to find our way.

Cayce repeatedly said that before too long America would face a complete economic breakdown, when those who could not engage the earth directly might suffer or starve. How a medical catastrophe (such as AIDS), a climate shift, or a nuclear disaster might bring this about is open to speculation. But the reason for taking on the primal growth process offered here is not survival of calamity, but survival of doubt. The sheer gift of the seasons, of things that know how to ripen in their time, is medicine for the soul of an anxious modern, uprooted by urban hustle and upset by personal crisis. Part of the process is remembering to bless particular plants and trees and creatures. A touch given with prayer to a lovely blossom, like a romp in the same spirit with a pet, creates channels for a life that knows the way of blessings, and enables us to receive blessings in turn.

Cayce took on the earth and nature to a degree that delighted those who knew him. All his adult life he planted and tended gardens, both for food (which he loved to can and preserve) and for the beauty of flowers and trees and shrubs. He constantly gave away shoots and seeds and bulbs, and swapped them with others. Buying from nursery catalogs absorbed him happily, and he was often bent over plants that needed his care. Perhaps not surprisingly, he reported that he could see little nature spirits among growing things; whether they helped him or not, some process did, for whatever he touched seemed to bloom ardently. Where he had the space he raised chickens, and kept the full range of pets, from dogs and cats to fish and birds. The out-of-doors called him in other ways—he sought huge ocean fish, or tramped fields and deserts and forests, ever eager to glimpse game. From this enterprise he drew a sense of the cycles of death and rebirth—so that he could make fresh starts when his activities crumbled, and so that he could die a little twice a day into a trance that nobody fully understood nor could guarantee would not cost him his life. Over and over he urged others to get close to the earth and its creatures, finding a glimpse of the living globe itself that must one day take the human family beyond war.

5. Become Involved with an Intentional Community

The next step is to make contact with a complete community of those who are seriously trying to build a better world. Starting such a community is a huge task, but visiting and helping to support one already going strong is within reach of anyone. It need not be residential, but it must be a community where people work together closely and patiently, under the impetus of an overarching ideal.

Contemporary life is so fragmented, and change seems driven mostly by special interests and private ambitions. Each of us deserves and can derive great benefit from the experience of sharing in life-renewing fellowship of a coherent community, building a new time and new ways. The A.R.E. Medical Clinic is such a community of like-minded (though often highly individualist) colleagues in the healing arts; and even the giant Mayo Clinic began as a physicians' cooperative on the Minnesota plains. Smaller and struggling communities often have the most to offer us, because our efforts to be appreciative and supportive can make an immediate difference to them.

Many Americans have found refreshment from the amazing achievements of Israeli communes, which try out new social and family patterns as they tame the dry and rocky land. Others have gone to the Findhorn Community in Scotland, finding not only outsize produce but outsize hearts and dreams of a better world, within a disciplined community. In other centuries, convents and abbeys and monasteries offered people engaged in living lives of purposeful relatedness the opportunity to work with the earth and with culture at the same time. Today the nearest example for many may be a small private college campus, trying to grow in grace and in truth at the same time; Waldorf and Montessori schools, which engage much more than rote learning; and art and music camps across the land (such as Interlaken in Michigan), where youth and elders join their efforts toward disciplined beauty. Settlement houses in cities can become beehives of creation full of the honey of self-respect, even for the underprivileged. Poets and therapists and shamans and philosophers have rallied to Esalen, in Northern California; as they have to its theologically inspired counterpart at the Institute for Creation-Centered Spirituality; or to Chinook Learning Center, on an island off the coast of Washington; or Interface, in urban Massachusetts. Whatever center we engage, the fullest participation involves praying for it by name, daily.

The adventure may start with a visit, or by subscribing to a periodical. When you find a promising adventurous group (none is ever perfect), then pitch in. You may enroll for days or weeks in a program (some of the best build housing for the poor in dilapidated city areas, as does the Church of the Savior in Washington, D.C., or the program of Habitat for Humanity). When personal circumstances limit this option, you may recruit and even sponsor others, particularly young people, to take part. Send something to the purpose-filled community regularly—money and, if possible, possessions. A useful idea is to subscribe twice to magazines or journals—once for yourself, and once for your adopted community.

Many a fellowship has a want list of needed equipment and books, and most of us have something we can spare that matches an item on the list, or can enlist friends to generate an item. Your first community need not be your last. Many have caught a vision from the Cayce-oriented A.R.E., for example, that later flowered in a medical center or a school or publishing venture—far away, under wholly different auspices. Indeed, part of the rhythm of life is finding when a lovely community should become a seedbed for growth, and not just a bed for our wearied spirits.

For Cayce, in small-town America of decades past, the church offered a fuller community than it often does today. The church was not for him a spare-time, weekend venture, but a major stream of life's creativity. It generated service projects, held discussions of social issues, taught the young, sponsored picnics and ball clubs, rescued the wounded, and sent helpers overseas or to slums. Cayce was never simply a devotee; he held major offices, led policy discussions, took on statewide responsibilities, and nurtured national figures with his friendship and his readings. He was not a crusading reformer, but he found ways to introduce new ideas and practices. He began with individuals, and their ideas have borne fruit in later generations—with a larger place for meditation in worship, with healing prayer, and with fresh views of human nature and history.

Cayce lived through two world wars, breadlines, and the age of concentration camps. Although his world often wounded him, it never broke his spirit—partly because he knew where community could be found and what it tasted like, so that ancient dreams from Israel and the early church were as real to him as the daily news, in their promise of things to come. When his readings affirmed that the hope of the world would emerge from Russia, as communism led to a larger vision of mutual responsibility, with room for the divine, he found the thought neither frightening nor unreasonable, because he knew intimately what determined community could generate.

6. Sponsor One Young Person's Education

Most of us get the opportunity to help the education of the young, usually our own offspring or those of relatives. But this next adventure involves picking somebody to whom we have no such commitment, chosen just for the joy of cocreating sponsorship. Don't do too much, just stay with one individual until the process is firm and clear, sending the creatures of doubt scuttling from your soul. Depending on your means, you may simply buy a good book now and then for the young person. If you pick someone in college, few gifts can be a richer invitation to an adventurous future than a journal in the field of the student's major, or sending the student to a professional conference in that same field. But you can satisfy simpler needs, such as clothing and desk supplies.

Some families find that their Christmas giving is better when it is focused on one young recipient, or a graduate student family, than strewn indiscriminately among relatives. Send cards, tapes, records, or art prints that you think will matter. The privilege of sending a young person on a trip of discovery—whether overseas, or to Washington, D.C., or to an anthropological dig—is one of life's sweet blessings. But it has its counterpart in just getting a youngster to a museum, a zoo, or a marine-life center. The best gifts carry a bit of ourselves, even when this means going where noisy youngsters overrun the place, or listening to a not-so-polished recital of piano students.

Giving some of ourselves is possible by a process not many consider, yet which can mean a great deal to a student: reading a paper that a struggling mind has prepared, or hearing a version of an oral report. Whether the student is in grade school, high school, or beyond, the prospect is the same. Having somebody other than a professor read a serious term paper is a gift of life to a weary graduate student; the next paper will go better because somebody cares.

Boosts like these are evident and precious. But not so evident is another process, which the young person may not even know about: praying for that individual by name, every day. Weeks, months, and even years of this kind of special sponsorship can become a remarkable process, probably as full of life for the one who prays—and thus becomes a partner with God—as the one who is prayed for. Prayers have a happy tendency to turn into phone calls, hugs, and notes, which make the pilgrimages of youth less frightening in an age that has forgotten how to mark rites of passage.

Cayce chose individuals for just such backing. Some were his missionary recruits; some were promising young people in his Sunday school classes; some he found in prisons or juvenile detention homes. More than once he spontaneously gave away his own well-marked Bible, used every day, to a youth whom he felt needed just that part of himself. Whenever he could, he hired young people to work for him, and gave them his empowering appreciation for their labor on his yard, on his studio, or on his fence. As a photographer, he took extra pains to make his portraits of young people shine with inner promise. Listening to his readings each day (as we often did) disclosed a lively pleasure in the counsel he offered the young, especially for those who were troubled or confused in their early years. Because his own youthful abilities to see the dead, discern auras, and memorize books marked him as different from his playmates, he had a special feeling for those who were shy and uncertain in their growing years. Reaching out to them helped to heal his old self-doubts, never completely gone in his strange vocation, and reminded him of God, whose love he most wanted to share in whatever he undertook.

7. Learn One Complete System of Thought

Systematic thought can do much to dissolve our doubts. The task of step 7 is to understand the full message of one serious thinker or school of thought. The system you choose should include a complete version of individual growth and change, or its breakdown, on the one hand; and social growth and change, or its breakdown, on the other. You may be able to learn this worldview in another way than by reading elaborate analyses and texts. One may find in the novels of Herman Melville, or the biography of Mahatma Gandhi, for example, more than teachings and tenets. Some will find reading all the plays or poetry of an author more rewarding than reading long discourses as such.

Whatever you choose, *system* is the key. Set down on paper the questions that an orderly vision of the human condition will address; the nature of truth and its proper discovery, the destiny of peoples and nations, and the character of beauty and justice and holiness. Keep expanding and refining the questions, so that they can become your own lifelong inquiries, starting with whatever system you take up.

The point of learning a complete system of thought is to be able to arrive at the big questions, which are only available to us if we travel the road of disciplined inquiry. Unfortunately, in our society, much of our information comes in little snippets. We keep up on topics by cannibalizing the culture with little bites of *Time*-sized reports, *Reader's Digest* briefings, or the headlines and television news. But we rarely try working with a coherent worldview. Thoughtful historians have noted that a large part of the world's people studies Marx systematically, and wonder whether the future may belong to these countries for the effort, not just for the doctrine.

The general guide to learning a system is to read all the major works of the author or authors; in the case of Jung or Freud or Marx, that can be a very large and technical assignment. There is no shame in using guidebooks (for example, the crisp little work on Jung by Calvin Hall, or the longer and wise statement by Edward Whitmont in *The Symbolic Quest*), nor even in using picture books with texts (*Man and His Symbols* is a visual feast of Jungian thought). But do not stop with these.

Ultimately there is no assurance that you have hold of your chosen system until you can explain it to others, and apply it to fresh challenges of behavior and policies, both personal and social. Participating in discussion groups becomes essential, even if these are play-reading groups that stop to think over a drama that has just been read aloud. Eventually the discussion process should lead to your presentations and speeches, for community or religious or special interest groups. Most of us can do much better than we think, when we put time into such a presentation—especially where others know less than we do!

It may seem strange, in a world of competing viewpoints and ideologies, to suggest that almost any coherent system that appeals to you will suffice as a starting place. At every step, however, you must conduct inquiry into *how* the system-maker knows—or claims to know—what is true and not true, and offers this for independent verification by others. Swallowing answers will only give you mental and moral indigestion, even if they be the best answers of our times or other times and cultures. Part of the system must be *method*, or examination of means for arriving at conclusions. Having done this work, more often than not you will find yourself branching out toward further systems that are more careful, more inclusive, or more useful for sharing with others.

In our culture, which reveals the loneliness of many of us by our preoccupation with gabble, we too easily sacrifice getting hold of a stout system for having "the latest" or the "inside dope." Merely having read topical articles or attended a conference is a poor substitute for seizing a system and living with it. Once you are well equipped, however, you will need to make comparisons, guess implications, and share your hunches with others interested in the same work. Only mad scientists think they can find truth alone.

To conclude that Cayce found his truth dripping from a nipple at his daily readings is to overlook his biography. It is clear that he had to grow into what he had, before his unconscious—in league with the Creative Forces—would give him a new type of reading. He had to sweat with each chapter of his concepts: his medical counsel opened into world affairs readings; then into astrology; on into geology; and eventually into history, reincarnation, dreams, small groups, and much more. Often it was only when he and his associates challenged his source to be clearer that they found something they could test in daily life, and make a part of their existence and community. It is no accident, in our view, that Cayce got much because he taught much; he was a gifted weekly Bible teacher for over half a century, and an able lecturer as well. The information that came through him got clearer and deeper as he figured out what he had that he could share with others.

The system Cayce most prized was biblical thought, with all its conflicting streams about life and death, truth and inspiration, morality and prudence. Unlike those who merely quote from the great scriptural storehouse, he studied it closely enough, with study aids of reading and of hearing great preaching, to grasp its central themes and work with them. Thus he was intimately aware of human evil and nobility, betrayal and life-rescuing sacrifice. To a later generation, struggling to find fresh faith and unhappy with what may seem hand-me-downs, Cayce's personal choice of a system may not do. But not everyone takes the trouble to work as hard with Sufism or Hinduism or Tibetan Buddhism as he did with his choice. Instead, we are all tempted to shop for ideas as if we were in a mall—picking up a little here and there, and proclaiming mindlessly that everyone is saying the same thing. This prevents us from perceiving the uniqueness of any system. The same temptation to skim follows us into psychology, anthropology, history, and politics. Not a few Jungians only pick up concepts and wear them, like accumulated merit badges, rather than putting on the full robes of Jung's thought, and walking where he walked until the trail leads onward.

Grappling with a cohesive worldview offers ways to think about our lot and our paths, and ways to communicate with others who also suffer uncertainty and panic. Happily, the worldview of the Cayce readings is itself slowly becoming a resource for systematic thinking, as more and more good books unpack it for claiming by disciplined effort. However, we can always fall into the trap of trying to grasp it without comparative study of Cayce's roots (so evident in his readings) in the great Western spiritual tradition; or of Eastern concepts such as kundalini, which spiral through the transcripts of his counseling sessions.

8. Help Prepare for a Birth

The final adventure of taming doubt, open to all of us, is a familiar human process that is given a fresh twist by the Cayce concept of reincarnation. In this view, souls choose their own births, in consultation with the Spirit and in some awareness of the general outlines of the life that will follow for them. Features of race, social class, education, employment, exposure to the elements, and illness, as well as concern with the arts or engineering or political struggles, all play into the soul's choice of family. Most often, the individual chooses a network of souls with which he or she has already worked, often as a family member, but often also as a member of a larger group taking on a social challenge.

Cayce saw the souls who incarnated in Colonial America as frequently having come from the ranks of the Crusades, so that they chose in the new colonies the very freedoms of faith and expression they had been too quick to take from others in an earlier century. In the same vein, he appeared to suggest in readings that the Spanish who suffered under Franco were in part those who had visited hardship on others when they exiled the Jews from Spain in 1492, and plundered lands in the New World. The perspective of the readings is that reincarnation is not blind retribution; but rather that it gives us the opportunity to learn, by choices that must be made in constricted circumstances, the very values that our souls demanded of others in earlier lifetimes. Tracing such interactions (including the likelihood that those who persecuted minorities in the past, or made them slaves, might incarnate in the same minority race or religion or gender in the present) did not mean, however, that present suffering could be ignored by others as simply what these souls deserved. Not to aid those in pain, whatever its origin, was to participate in the sin of neglect, which could bring its own harship to those who merely observed what they should have tried to change for their fellows.

At the present time, Cayce's sweeping vistas of karma must remain largely conjecture. But nestled in among these is a challenge that many have taken up, in the more than sixty years since Cayce's readings first began systematically developing a viewpoint of reincarnation within Western faith. It is the invitation to prepare for a birth, every few years—whether as parent or relative, or as friend and companion in faith. The process of inviting in a soul, while by no means mechanical, was described in the Cayce readings as sufficiently lawful to justify concerted effort by those who would welcome its arrival. By giving special attention and dedication to definite values and interests, a family and its associates might pull in a like-minded and ample soul—not simply for the joy of a ride through life together, but also for larger service. The quality of parenting, supported by ambient good will and high purpose, could make a place for a soul of high intelligence, humor, or talents, needed in the human family just now.

Accordingly, many couples have gone fishing in the sea of souls by undertaking definite disciplines during pregnancy, and committing themselves to carry these farther into rearing the new child. Their intent has not been to master a realm of studies, but rather to dedicate themselves and the yet unborn to larger ideals, larger outcomes, just as biblical figures from Hannah to Elizabeth and Mary offered their new offspring to the Lord. These couples—with their present children and with available and interested grandparents, aunts, and uncles—have followed impressions from dreams and from prayer to prepare themselves for the birth of a gifted soul, if that be God's will.

Parents readying themselves for a child responsive to music have listened to music and sung it and talked about it; others have engaged in reading and action on political themes or ecological concerns or medical motifs. Sometimes they have reported psychically seeing the faces and feeling the force of the children to come, while the fetus is still in the womb. Gladys McGarey, M.D., who has specialized in obstetrics and gynecology, has reported on these delightful experiences in her book *Born to Win*, where Cayce motifs have guided not only her patients' but her own visions. It is important to remember that these seekers for new souls have not tried to impose their will on the child, but to let the final answer come from the new soul and from God. For example, although all parents wish for a healthy child, a particular family might need a handicapped person, both for its own growth and for the growth of the rest of the family unit. With the earnest effort to prepare a lighted path for a promising and talented soul must go the commitment to welcome whatever soul arrives, and to choose it fully.

As always in the Cayce picture, regular prayer is an important part of this pre-birthing and birthing process. The spirit should be one of dedication, not claiming spiritual privilege. But prayer needs reinforcing with treasures of nature, poetry, friends, artifacts from loved cultures, drawings, and dance, until the loveliness of the longing in parents' hearts is matched by the lovely surroundings and interactions into which the soul might be drawn. Those who have entered into the process for months, and followed and aided the newborn afterwards—as "Godparents" in a very full sense—report that the process has been profoundly refreshing in itself, reminding them of all the fresh starts and great surprises that life offers. So this project brings its tender fruits even to those who are uncertain about reincarnation.

Assigning famous past lives to people who got readings was not typical of the Cayce counsel. The readings seemed fully mindful of the ego traps involved, and selected with care which lifetimes should be mentioned and which kept aside. Even Cayce was not informed of what became a pivotal lifetime for his own self-understanding until fifteen years after others were spelled out, because—he was told—learning that he had been the head of a church in Laodicea in New Testament times, and a follower of Jesus in Galilee before that, would have made him "puffed up" with self-importance. Only after he went through cleansing heartbreak and forgave colleagues who turned away from him or against him was his soul scoured enough to receive this profoundly meaningful information.

Yet there were some instances where newborn children were designated in his readings as having great promise. One was described as having been Franz Liszt; another a founder of a Protestant church tradition; and yet another—for whom there had been much preparation—as having been both Alexander the Great and Thomas Jefferson. The lot of these children growing up with such knowledge or claims from Cayce was not always easy, and even seemed at times counterproductive. Yet the Cayce source offered the vision of their promise, as part of its assurance that noble, gifted souls could be drawn in as large adventures of service, for those willing to take the responsibility. Again and again these readings insisted that a stable, loving family life was absolutely crucial for the realization of the promise that a gifted soul might bring. Otherwise the same talents that might provide leadership could become energies twisted into mental illness.

This project is an appropriate way to end the list, because it is so lovely and personal that it balances off the trying demands of the others. No thoughtful person will be surprised to consider that entering into the total birthing process with loved companions can hold off the demons of doubt, both doubt of self and doubt of the ever-renewed goodness of the divine.

6

Where Did God Go?
Understanding Karma
and Reincarnation

In Christopher Fry's free-verse play, *A Sleep of Prisoners*, the three sleep-walking and sleep-acting prisoners—dreaming together that they are Shadrac, Meshac, and Abednego—find themselves joined in the fiery furnace by the fourth prisoner, also dreaming the plot. He is the one whom the Bible identifies in its story as an angel, but in the play he speaks of himself only as "Man" in God's service. In an impassioned speech, which wakens them all and brings the drama toward its close, he links suffering and wrong directly to growth Godward:

> Thank God our time is now when wrong
> Comes up to face us everywhere,
> Never to leave us till we take
> The longest stride of soul men ever took.
> Affairs are now soul size.
> The enterprise
> Is exploration into God.

When cruel blows strike, most of us ask sooner or later how our suffering relates us to God, or whether God even cares or can respond. Can the fiery pain of loss and wrong really burn off bonds that keep us from our destined freedom, and win us soul size that leads directly "into God"?

Glib answers will not do. Sooner or later we need to ask not only how we can resolve the crisis creatively, when our old habits are scalded off by hot tears, but how we are meant to transform as individuals these outrageous events into something worthwhile.

In this chapter, we will explore the answer given by the Cayce resource to one of the oldest questions human beings ask when confronted by brutalizing crisis: "Where did God go?" (If your shock and grieving are still fresh and raw, you might want to skip this chapter and come back to it later. The issues are not simple, and Cayce's views can be easily misunderstood, especially if your mind is dulled by pain.) According to the Cayce view, the answer is karma. In casual use, "karma" too often suggests a system of punishment or impersonal retribution, and therefore compounds the agony of the wounded heart. As we shall see, however, karma in the Cayce view is neither punitive nor blind justice. It is instead a process of steady, divine love meant to stretch us in particular ways, congruent with the pregnancy and delivery of the complex.

THE PROBLEM OF UNJUST SUFFERING

Rabbi Harold Kushner, in his compassionate book *When Bad Things Happen to Good People*, tells of his soul-searing struggle with faith when his young son slowly died of a hopeless disease. His final answer to the question, "Where did God go?" is that God is right beside sufferers—caring for them, helping, and growing them, but powerless to prevent or stop certain kinds of unjust suffering.

That answer is one of several that people of deep faith have reached. It is not, however, the answer of the Cayce readings. These extraordinary counseling discourses shine with assurance of the same divine compassion that Kushner sees, but they look in a different direction. Here even the harshest events are within the mercy and providence of God, in a universe built to free sleeping prisoners for the ultimate exploration, as cocreators headed Godward.

For centuries, thoughtful individuals in crisis have tried to make three affirmations. They cannot all be true at once, though each seems to the hungry and wounded spirit to have merit:

1. God is all-powerful, able to create, sustain, and guide a good universe and meaningful human existence. God's awesome power is self-limited to give humans enough freedom to exercise serious choices, making them worthy bearers of the divine image and potential; but it is accompanied by enough ultimate wisdom to allow God to see the larger consequences of creation and human choices, so as to limit stupid hardship.
2. God is just and loving toward humans, without fail or flaw, although his/her purposes and presence may often elude sufferers for a time.
3. Humans experience unjust suffering and evil, which such a God would prevent. However large the segment of untoward happenings that wayward humans deserve, a portion of the human lot remains utterly and finally unfair and unloving.

Stuck with this riddle, philosophers, theologians, and just plain bereft spouses and parents, as well as besieged soldiers and the handicapped, have tried reformulating each of the three affirmations to make the whole package work.

Some have insisted that God is not all-powerful or supremely wise, but still an immensely creative force for good, doing what he/she can with an evolving cosmos that is sometimes intractable and darkly harsh toward humans. This cosmos may be all God's creation, but it has somehow gotten out of hand; or perhaps it is a Given that God did not create, but found loose in the universe. Whatever the case, the divine needs human aid to handle it, so that the outcome may one day be coherent order in the universe, toward which the holy strives. This view, sometimes called the "doctrine of the suffering God," has found wise and sensitive modern exponents. Rabbi Kushner is one of these. The problem with this solution is that it offers limited assurance that God is the final reality, since the Given may be greater. The grounds for utter allegiance from human hearts appear to many to be undercut by this position. One might seek to help God, but be tempted to hedge final bets.

Others have tried affirming that what humans know of love and justice cannot always be attributed to God, whose stupendous might and vital energy may not be dependably loving toward humankind. Carl Jung appears to take this position in *The Answer to Job*, an impassioned and not easily read book, which he wrote in two weeks while suffering from a fever. Whether he is speaking there of the ultimate reality (which he refuses to speculate about in his other books) or of the evolving archetype of the divine in Western faith is open to debate. In any case, he ascribes to what humans encounter as God a "dark" side. This dark side is not fully moral, because the divine has not consulted itself and its native omniscience as to the consequences of its actions—such as allowing Satan (as a kind of mysterious presence in God) to afflict Job with terrible undeserved loss and illness.

In Jung's view, influential in some psychological circles, Job's own cry to God against God (which might be any sufferer's cry in crisis) awakens a just and loving response. It is the sending of the Christ, as the first step toward fulfillment of the divine imperative to become human, which it longs to do out of its creative nature (as the Word becoming flesh), not only in the Christ but in everyone. The authors are among those who read Jung's visionary and burning essay as an account of the unfolding God archetype in the collective unconscious. But insofar as this or any view suggests that God is not fully loving and fair, it undercuts devotion and commitment in crucial ways, although it makes sense of certain kinds of impenetrable misfortune.

Finally, some have tried to lessen or remove the claim that humans experience unjust suffering or evil, whatever appearances and circumstance may indicate. Certain medieval theologians proposed that God might be lovingly running the cosmos for the benefit of the angels, not for humans at all. Thornton Wilder suggests in *The Bridge of San Luis Rey* that our individual suffering and loss (like the sudden deaths of his travelers on the collapsing bridge) contribute blood-bright threads to a tapestry of God's creation much larger than we can imagine. Some have recently wondered whether life spinning along in other galaxies might be more important to God than ours, requiring processes that unfortunately hurt earthlings. Others have tried assigning meaningless individual pain to social causes, where the human family oftens lays the foundations for personal tragedy. Many have viewed personal deprivation as the testing and cleansing of faith, to be rewarded after death. Each such solution comes close to the peril of denying God's unflagging love and justice, or God's potency to activate that love in dire circumstances. Yet this solution of challenging the appearance of unjust suffering is the one most often chosen, rightly or wrongly, by those of deep faith within religious history. Cayce's readings belong here.

The Cayce counsel supports the viewpoint of a large segment of the human family (notably Hinduism and Buddhism, but also minority voices in other traditions, including historic Judaism, Islam, and Christianity). His readings say that what seems unjust suffering is actually the fair and steady final lawfulness of the universe, reflecting the consequences of actions taken in previous lives (the word karma means "action"), in forms that will lead the soul onward to a very large destiny.

The discerning reader will note that while this position resolves the immediate riddle of the three conflicting affirmations, it does not necessarily explain why suffering must exist in the workings of the cosmos. It deals with justice better than with love. Could not a truly loving God have fashioned a better design?

KARMA AS LOVE: THE CAYCE VIEW OF CREATION AND HUMAN DESTINY

The Cayce readings ultimately leave love as a mystery we can fully know *only* by participating in it with God, when we no longer see "as in a glass, darkly." They describe a cosmos dancing with compassion, even while it operates with unfailing lawfulness. "Love is Law, as Law is Love" is a typical affirmation. This is not just an epigram, but a claim to describe the bones of reality. In this view, God created all souls at the same time: in the beginning, when God, whose nature is Love, found that such caring required companionship. The divine intent was not to allow needless hurt to any soul, each of whom was equally precious to God. No predestination of the elect and the damned appears here, for (in a combination of scripture verses often cited in the readings) "God hath not willed that any soul should perish, but hath with every temptation provided a means of escape." The divine created a universe that contained cures for every ailment (though not necessarily for every particular illness or injury); resources for every hardship; companionship for every loneliness; survival for every human death. Above all, it was fashioned to nurture growth of souls, which were made in the image of God and destined to be God's conscious collaborators, however long this might require.

Such growth required that vast freedom be given to souls—but freedom within a structure of order and limits, which would patiently teach them their nature and destiny, rather than simply allow them license. They had to be permitted free will for major choices, even if some of these decisions, like those of the Prodigal Son, led to chastening privation and hardship. In the Cayce view (which must be treated as a visionary effort toward a hypothesis, nothing more), not all souls chose the earth as a sphere for their growth. Those who did so found it easy, in the beginning, to play and toy with earth's creatures. But in the process, some lost their inner connection with the divine, and lost their balance in the interplay of matter and spirit by choosing self-indulgence at the expense of their greater unfolding. The problem was not earth, which was fair in God's eyes and a fitting garden for soul growth (this is not a dualistic outlook, where matter is necessarily inferior, nor a trap to be escaped); the problem was imagination and will given untutored autonomy. So a limiting and lawful way had to be created. This way would allow souls immediate access to the divine, if they chose to learn its requirements; yet it would also teach them the true nature of existence, both through worthwhile achievements and through the suffering that might follow their excesses—not as punishment, but as education.

The human pilgrimage through successive lives was the design. It was meant to selectively activate "patterns" (Cayce's term for archetypes) from the immense God-spun treasury of resources inherent in every soul and human body. Souls had to learn proportion and priorities, test values, use and misuse energies. Only in this way could the souls return to their original Oneness with the divine source, now "conscious of same"—a qualitative gain for all creation.

As in Jung's thought, consciousness is the great prize. It means that the soul must not only recognize God and obey God's lawfulness, but finally "become the Law" in the deepest recesses of the mind and will and spirit—even though this process might require eons to accomplish. Souls that became the divine law could (to paraphrase Augustine's terse Latin) love and do as they liked. In their loving—and yet more loving—they would enter into utter unison (though not identity) with love itself, and desire only what expressed this condition. According to the readings, the intent of reincarnation and its vital dynamics of karma was to yield souls that would be "one with the All, yet not that All."

This view contains a version of the Fall from grace, but it is not an account of drastic alienation that produces souls utterly unworthy of God's love but given that love anyway. Rather, it tells of souls awakening from slumbering innocence—a sleep of the self-imprisoned, perhaps—into responsible maturity, within the round of earthly journeys. Elaborating that journey to maturity, the Cayce viewpoint describes (as did both the ancient Stoics and Rudolph Steiner) a series of between-life sojourns in realms of consciousness quite different from earth, which give the soul gifts of temperament and interest and values to enrich its earthly journeys. Finally, the Cayce picture stretches the journey of the soul far beyond earthly existence of any kind. It continues to grow in spheres only hinted at, in imagery that suggests fashioning and redeeming worlds or realms unguessed.

Although this picture is unusual for Western faith, it may be seen as in some ways an extension of the long-held (but now often discarded) concept of purgatory, in that it affirms the continued growth of souls beyond one earthly lifetime. Yet it differs from familiar versions of purgatory in presenting after-death existence as more than trials and purgative pain. Instead it describes the privilege of each incarnation as being the kind of companionship and growth Jesus intended when he spoke (John 10:10) of bringing "life and that more abundantly." It also differs from some Eastern versions of karma. The soul does not enter into animal bodies, nor climb the ladder of caste toward escape from the regrettable wheel of rebirth.

In the Cayce view, the drama of each lifetime is seen in fully human terms: closeness to God is not simply a destination, but an increasingly present reality. We find it by keeping the great commandments of attunement and service, in any station or position or affliction. Because the purpose of this huge pilgrimage is to incarnate love, souls might complete their needed earthly schooling, and yet want to return in the flesh to help their fellows and the larger creation. For such love is greater than grades of attainment.

Here Cayce's cosmic mural approaches the Buddhist vision of the highly evolved Bodhisattva, who forswears absorption into Nirvana until every blade of grass can attain it also. But the image in the Cayce materials is typically expressed in the Western answer of Jesus, when asked why a man had been born blind—was it his parents' sin or his own (in a kind of karma)? The ringing answer in John 9:3, which put the emphasis on all such causation of suffering as purposeful, not punitive, was neither, but that the works of God might be manifested. Karma can only be understood as love in action.

One way to grasp the Cayce perspective on reincarnation would be to ask someone deeply pledged and tutored in married love what difference to that love it would finally make, were one to learn that a spouse had once been mentally ill, or jailed, or adopted, or greatly talented, or secretly wealthy, or for that matter previously married. Full love, however astonished, would finally only ask what helpful fruits might be grown from the experience, now or in the future. So it would be with reincarnation, in the Cayce view. Not who we have been, but who we are and can become, is the intent and gift of karma.

REINCARNATION: FIGURE AND GROUND IN FAITH

The novelty of the perspective of reincarnation for the Western mind inevitably commands attention. The Cayce readings, however, set the process of purposeful rebirth in a view of human nature and destiny that differs surprisingly little in its major outlines from historic biblical faith. It is easy to give reincarnation as a figure so much attention that it loses its ground or context in the larger drama of soul growth. For the Cayce readings, all the great themes—sin and grace, covenant and redemption, blessing and sacrifice, obedience and wisdom, reason and revelation, creation and celebration, overcoming selfishness and doing justice—are still the essential concerns, whether examined in one lifetime or many.

Christ remains the decisive pattern and resource in the Cayce readings. He is both the model for all souls, in his utter Oneness with the Father, and the bearer of ever-renewing aid. God finds joy in other religious traditions than the Christian, and blesses their special gifts; yet the readings stress that the one called variously Logos and Son and Light is still descriptive of the ultimate reality humans need to engage. "He is your karma" is a pregnant phrase from the Cayce materials.

What do the Cayce readings add to mainstream Western faith? In some respects, nothing, as careful reading of the rich biblical references in these readings will show. Yahweh is seen as keeping his promises, as of old, and ever ready to respond to a contrite and generous heart. He is seen as empowering communities of loving, working, and faith. These communities are not self-serving, but seek "to do justly, to love mercy, and to walk humbly with thy God." Cayce's positive, rather than punitive, emphasis on the scheme of reincarnation does not, however, reduce the danger that goes with every view of human nature that places it very close to the divine nature: hubris, inflation, and self-authoring. Here the Cayce warning is severe: "All have sinned and fallen short."

The efforts of the individual to grow Godward are precious to the divine. These would not be productive if tried apart from nurturing others ("We only get into heaven leaning on the arm of those we have helped"); and they would be drastically slowed if attempted as good works for merit, rather than in faithful humility that understands and seeks the selfless way of the one called the Christ ("He alone bore it all," for "There is only one Master"). The Cayce readings spoke sharply of other dangers in misusing the viewpoint of reincarnation: putting off moral responsibility to another life; leaving others in misery as their personal lot; escaping into egotism over the famous or impressive person one once was; and looking back for causes at the expense of gazing ahead to purposes.

For those who find the whole notion of reincarnation peculiar (and the idea of being one's own ancestor, as well as destined to be one's own descendant, is not a little strange), it may help to recall that each generation or epoch shapes its own understanding of the nature-nurture controversy. The hypothesis of reincarnation may be seen as only the latest in a weighty sequence of shifts of Western viewpoint. The suggestion that we carry the cumulative talents and energies and riddles of prior existences right into our daily lives, screened by chosen purposes in this lifetime, is not necessarily more outrageous than other generations found Charles Darwin's notion that our bodies have participated in the whole chain of evolution. Nor is it more preposterous than arguing, with Karl Marx, that economic forces determine our history and prospects more than it might appear; or asserting, with Sigmund Freud, that the patterns of infancy run decisively through adult life. All are components of our existence not easily inspected; yet they are thinkable and useful once we have postulated and investigated them. To suggest that all of us have lived on earth before, and carry influential patterns and dynamics because of our prior choices and efforts, only extends the concept of the unconscious through time.

But plausibility does not define truth. For us to think of rebirth as real, and not just an interesting fancy, we need to account for several mediating processes, none of which are yet well established. For example, since bodies are so deeply intertwined with character, we have to conceive how a soul might move from one to another without becoming utterly different. The Cayce viewpoint suggests that souls choose carefully, to find which bodies (and families) will fit their nature and purposes. They then modify these bodies toward the proper individuality by acting on a "finer physical body," which interpenetrates the flesh and especially interacts with the endocrine glands through the chakras.

All of this is still hypothesis, with elusive component processes. For souls to learn and grow through successive earthly (and between-earthly) sojourns, we have to suppose a form of memory that transcends time (presumably operating with psychic capacities); and a deep center of being that compares past and present in the light of a potential future. Some psychologists, such as Jung, postulate a Self that might do all this; others postulate a "tertiary process" in the psyche that complements the better-known "primary process" of dream and wish and drive, and the "secondary process" of outward adjustment and skills.

For reincarnation to make sense, we must further propose that souls make responsible free choices within limits—otherwise karma is merely a regrettable residue from a random chain of events. We also have to imagine a nonaccidental universe, which organizes events so as to bring needed and just opportunities to each individual, even in such complex social events as war and floods. This is a staggering challenge. Finally, we have to picture how growth can occur, a little at a time, on thematic lines, so that fortunate and unfortunate events alike build both creative potency and enlarged personhood. In this book we have used the concept of the growth episode or complex for that purpose.

We can draw a little encouragement for the task of investigating reincarnation if we recognize that the processes by which forgotten childhood patterns crucially influence adult behavior are likewise elusive (though we assume that these are discoverable). And we know even less about what Freud called "the choice of the neurosis," in which two children of the same family and general upbringing develop distinctive styles of both effectiveness and collapse. As Stanislav Grof and other investigators of the unconscious have suggested, the influences of past lives may provide the missing piece that makes such divergence thinkable, in that children may start life predisposed to react in certain ways both to traumas and to happy circumstances.

THE PERSONAL CRISIS AS KARMA

In the Cayce view, much more is carried over from lifetime to lifetime than predisposition to misfortune and pain. Quoting a New Testament letter, his readings often insisted that "God is not mocked; whatsoever a man soweth, that shall he also reap." This does not imply a mechanical balancing of ledgers, although "The Law of the Lord is perfect, converting the soul," and "Ye shall pay every whit" for that which has been wrongly done or left undone. Instead, "God looks on the heart" so that *intent*, rather than a list of artificially specified sins or neatly arranged attainments, is the measure of actions.

Yet all that we mean by poetic justice, felicitous or regrettable, is to be found in the accounts of four or five past lifetimes apiece (chosen from many more, because of their special relevance to the present), which Cayce traced in some detail for some 2,500 people, in "life readings" given over a period of two decades. Most of these reports cannot be verified, although they can be compared with the subjective impressions and present-life histories of surviving recipients and those close to them.

Cayce's account of reincarnation gives primary attention to four clusters of karma crucial to our humanness: talents, texture, spirituality, and opportunities. Let us consider each one in some detail, exploring how they may carry over from one lifetime to another, and may even be among the root causes of our present personal crises.

Karma of Talents

In the Cayce view, talents and abilities developed in earlier lifetimes by rigorous application and generous sharing are likely to pop up again. The talents traced in life readings ran through several past lifetimes (we have deliberately simplified the patterns here, for purposes of illustration):

- A woman, who trained maturing girls for marriage in ancient Egypt, returned as a gifted and patient minister, often working with couples before and during marriage.
- A nurse, who tended the battle-wounded with loving care, returned with her own body beautiful enough for use in modeling.
- A trader in ancient Persia was reborn with skills that made him a success at the rental-car business.

- A craftsman and trader in woods and metals used these talents to develop a veritable business empire of radio cabinets (which he did at Cayce's suggestion).

People who were now, or could become, inventors, physicians, writers, stockbrokers, psychics, farmers, sports reporters, athletes, or artists, or could claim the one vocation that Cayce saw as unexcelled—rearing children—were each shown in readings that their particular talents, interests, knacks, skills, and abilities had been developed in prior existences.

Similarly, talents misused in the past could bring serious problems in the present, some of which would result in personal crises:

- A lovely girl coerced by her parents to seduce and spy in the American Revolution was now back as an epileptic, who required constant attention from the very same parents.
- A nobleman in the French Revolution, who had closed his ears to cries for help then, was deaf in this life.
- A minister in Colonial America, who had used his position and abilities to "duck" in water those wrongly suspected of witchcraft, was troubled in this life with chronic bedwetting.
- A healer with the power to affect the flesh used his ability instead to move cards and peas under shells as gambling targets, fleecing Indians and settlers on the American frontier. He was back now without the power, and chronically out of money.
- A harsh literary critic from another time found himself handicapped by drastic self-doubt in the present.

Clearly, karma of talents can create crises in the present. Yet the Cayce view does not present karma as meaningless hardship, simply to be endured while the soul broods inwardly on its mistakes. Instead, karma is meant to set in motion a dynamic of growth and change.

Essentially, the workings of painful karma, as contrasted with felicitous karma, were presented by Cayce as the working out of complexes across time. The individual soul would circle around certain defined themes in ways that required attention, patience, and disciplined effort. Karma constricts one's focus and gathers one's energy—not for death, but for new life. Narrowing of effort and energy, whether in death loss, blocked opportunity, or blows of illness and injury, is meant to fire the psyche to insights, energy, richer values, larger personhood, and more fruitful relationships with God and one's fellows—precisely the gifts of archetypes that are the core of complexes.

Karma of Texture

The texture of the self that carries over from life to life is richly woven, in the Cayce view. Impulses, interests, aspirations, defenses, attractions, antipathies, inhibitions, health patterns, and appetites all show up—some of them greatly influenced by between-life sojourns in realms of beauty or intelligence or forcefulness or some other primary quality. Part of texture is the capacity to learn and change, to come under discipline, to refer daily experience to larger principles and commitments. Deep emotions and the triggers that release them—sexuality, anger, compassion, self-pity, hate—carry over from life to life.

Some of this individual legacy of texture is positive:

- A man, who had taught the Law of God with Joshua, came back with it as an intuitive guide to his college teaching of psychology.
- An inspired emissary from England to William Penn returned as a gifted British diplomat in the present, able to discern the eternal in ordinary transactions.
- A ruler in ancient Egypt returned with the confidence and authority to build an international corporation.
- A deeply feminine woman, who had never incarnated as a man, came back as lover and helper to a gifted man who needed her as a secretary.
- A generous mother in ancient Israel found that she had the resources to help a schizophrenic son today.

Yet texture, too, can be problematic:

- A man, who had developed high intuitive wisdom in ancient Persia, returned with unresolved questions about loving too many women; his wisdom needed to be tempered with caring.
- A woman, who had been an entertainer, sacrificing her artistry to the pleasure of others, came back longing to dance but chained to a desk as a secretary.
- A young woman, who had jeered at Christians ripped open by animals in the Roman gladiatorial arena, returned with tuberculosis of the hip that required her to learn how pain needs compassion.
- A man, who ridiculed homosexuals in the French court, came back with unbridled homosexual appetites.
- A woman, who mocked the overweight in Rome, developed as painfully obese in the present.

In the Cayce view, we are each required to experience the behavior we demanded intemperately of others. Our standards become our ideals, and what shapes karma is individual ideals and what we do about them. Souls are not held to an arbitrary universal mold, but to the full implications of what they themselves choose.

As with talent, so with texture. The emergence of personal crises from past excesses or indifference is not merely sad retribution. It is not debts to be paid. The only one to pay is oneself. Most growing through stressful karma requires giving to others the worthwhile things we want for ourselves. The others might even be the same parent or child or spouse as in the past, or stand in some reversal of roles. The challenge is not the cast of characters, but the inner plot. We do not have karma to work out with individuals tossed into our lives, although past actions may draw them to us "for weal or for woe." We have to ride the horse of karma to a farther place than settling accounts; the course is full growth.

Karma of Spirituality

The style or manner of spirituality, or trusting relationship to God, is a crucial part of karmic legacies. This relationship often governs the progress of all others, and one's inner becoming, in life after life. According to the Cayce readings, the heart of spirituality is a lively, risking, imaginative, grateful style of daily cocreating with the divine. For the person who walks close to God, this means ever seeking to empower others, to free them from their needless bonds, to educate and to link them in worthwhile causes. We must do all this with the sensitivity born of regular attunement and real listening to others as well as listening to nature, and receiving the gifts of the arts and ceremony. To maintain such a cocreating style, we must make promises or vows; but we must also be open to reworking these vows as wisdom, grace, and kindness grow in the soul. These promises are covenants, as we have seen. Yet keeping covenants leads to specific disciplines, the depth of discipleship, in humility and in confidence, within the company of the nobly like-minded.

In Cayce's readings, karma in spirituality can be a great blessing, brought naturally from another life:

- Cayce was himself described in the readings as having brought his own spiritual judgment (which kept him modest, despite his striking attainments) from a past lifetime as the leader of a Laodicean church in New Testament times.
- A priestess, who inspired many to large worldviews and ethical lives in ancient Atlantis, was back (according to a life reading) with the capacity to inspire the same as a lecturer in countries all around the globe—which she did.
- A woman, who gave depth to Chinese spiritual teachings as an empress, returned to be an American missionary to China in this lifetime, and then a teacher of prayer who drew on many cultures for her writing and training.
- A Roman courtesan, whose large spirit helped her to befriend early Christians, returned as a researcher in spiritual teachings today.
- An Egyptian priest, who had introduced choral singing into temple worship of an ancient time, returned with a gift for sacred choral conducting. This gift took him to churches and campuses alike, interpreting not only scores but the text.
- A teacher at the time of Israel's return from Exile returned with

a gift for seeing universals in philosophy, though his vocation was in business.

The karma of spirituality can also produce problems and crises. What we trust might have to be stretched by suffering:

- A man, who had not trusted his wife's love when he left her for the Crusades, and put her in a painful chastity belt, was married to her in this life; but he was unable to enjoy sex, despite her sensuous beauty, because she was chronically angry at him.
- Some who trusted in the might of Rome and taunted Christian martyrs returned crippled with polio.
- Some who trusted in their own might had enslaved African natives, and then returned as modern blacks to lives of limited circumstances.

Again and again, this pattern emerged from the readings: what one gives to others in the name and spirit of God will return, often manyfold; what is withheld—even while chanting that same name—will be withheld in turn. Yet the intent of karma seems to be to awaken a spirit of larger creativity, not to drag down a victim of little-remembered deeds:

- One who mocked those killed by gladiators in Rome used her now-awakened passion for sufferers to help her recall how to play the harp, which in time lifted the spirits of many in concert halls.
- A wastrel, who seduced women on the American frontier and left them with babies, returned deeply concerned about abandoned children, and made children the core of his medical practice.

Even the harshest betrayal of the divine, leading to suffering, can be completely turned around if trust is put in the one who showed on the Cross how to bring every circumstance to God, even cruel death. Meditation and prayer, in a life that blossoms with service, can turn the panicked heart toward steady paths of renewal and growth.

Karma of Opportunities

Finally, Cayce claimed that opportunities also carry over from life to life. Those who served well in leadership, healing, music, education, business, or science would be expected to have opportunities to do so again. Some souls, however, might deliberately choose to walk a path of limited circumstance and means, in order to know how the neglected of the world lived:

- A Roman official, who taught state games, came back as a banker, who loved baseball and got to play it well.
- An Egyptian embalmer, who served his people with skill, returned to the opportunities of a gifted osteopath, with a talent for herbs.
- A general in the ranks of Alexander the Great was reborn with opportunities to lead students well in campus upheavals.

Those who used fully and fruitfully the opportunities of love and marriage and parenting would find these connections open to them again, while those who cared for their bodies responsibly, and helped others to do so, found blessings of good health and attractive mien. Opportunities are not unmixed blessings, however. Holding political power, professional leadership, and marital responsibility are all fraught with decisions crucial to soul growth. Only the opportunity is assured, not the outcome.

Taking opportunities from others means the likelihood of reduced options for one's own later life:

- A medieval chemist, who made potions that injured or poisoned others, returned with allergies that limited his opportunities.
- A Mayan leader, who had spilled much blood in ritual ceremonies, came back anemic—restrained by the weakness in his own blood from things he would like to do.
- A dissolute Japanese woman, daughter of an American sailor, returned in an unhappy marriage where her husband gave her a life-restricting venereal disease from his affairs.

But none of these circumstances was meant to operate as punishment, only as focusing.

Over and over the Cayce readings insist, "Start with what you have in hand, and the next will be given to you." Even the severe limitations of a retarded, handicapped, or bedridden person can be split open by smiles and kind words, until the hardship becomes a wellspring of blessings to those nearby. According to the readings, the principle in any walk of life is to act on the resources, inner and outer, which are presently available. Doing so activates archetypes, whose growth equips the person to see patterns unguessed before. At the same time, the living Spirit, "bearing witness with thy spirit," brings helpers and openings. "Like attracts like" is a primal law of the universe, in the Cayce perspective.

Is the crisis that bewilders rooted in our karma? Cayce's perspective says that it can be, though it need not be. Aging and death, for example, are appointed to the human condition, partly to allow the merciful forgetting of inadequate lifetimes, so that we can make fresh starts. The visitation of these patterns need not be harsh individual karma, but merely part of the privileges of being human. In the same way, life's small deaths—moving away, starting a new school, quitting the field of lovers for one steady spouse, attaining less than we hope on an exam or a sales project—need not be invested with cosmic soul import. Indeed, the secret for all distresses, little or large, normal or abnormal, is the life "hid with Christ in God." This is not meant to be mere theological assent or moral conformity, but hearty participation in the human lot—"today, now" with the purpose of being "a channel of blessings to others."

Down such streambeds can flow all the energies and wisdom of creation, as seen in the adventures of Edgar Cayce. As he did, any of us may choose to make ourselves ever more available to those who need us in our round of life—not by self-obliteration (for God ever seeks defined and mature selfhood), but by "self-bewilderment in Him." Then there may occur to us, from springs as deep as creation itself, what is needed for the crisis at hand, and how to stand taller in the days of our years.

EXPLORING KARMA WITH DREAMS

Although Cayce gave readings to help people in distress locate and deal better with their own karma, he consistently offered suggestions on how they could find similar patterns for themselves. He and his readings did not want devotees, nor did they want to encourage styles of seeking channels and revealers in every occult or New Age publication or gathering. The readings advised that it is better to turn within for intuitive guidance and discovery. After all, what is offered by another—be it plucked from telepathy or the ether or the Akashic Record (a term from Sanskrit to suggest vibrations left by past lives on strands of time and space)—has still to be evaluated by oneself. Sound guidance on past lives and karma can only be given to those who already in principle have it, or can find it for themselves.

Dreams are one resource often suggested by the Cayce readings, but they are not the only way to connect with the buried past. All of the recommended procedures must be used for growth and service, not mere amazement. With resolve less than the best, one will get fanciful imagery trips from the unconscious, but rarely reliable insights and recall. Given a wholesome intent, however, and a firm pledge to use or act on what emerges as helpful, anyone can rightfully explore the legacies of particular past lives. The karmic themes run through several existences right into tomorrow's health, job opportunities, and faith choices—indeed, into any sphere of authentic human existence.

The Cayce readings subordinate the discernment of particular past existences, with locale and vocation and associates for each, to the purpose for such discovery. But since past-life recall (in this view) typically occurs at points of decision and major growth, the Cayce readings did not hesitate to identify some dream material (for most people, a small amount of their dreams) as illuminative remembering.

Literal fragments of memory are often embedded in larger dream sequences. Certain indicators can alert us to this material. Among the sixty-seven dreamers for whom Cayce gave his major dream interpretations, he singled out past languages being spoken in dreams as Hebrew, Egyptian, and Persian. Among the images he identified as actual recall were a desert oasis, a huge and threatening Arabian bending over a dreamer, the tents of Israelites coming back from Babylon, rays and machines from Atlantis, fishing on the Sea of Galilee, the ceremonial dedication of an Egyptian pyramid, death by combat in a Greek arena, the landing of ships in early America, Roman rule of Mediterranean lands, the spreading of Hindu thought outside India, and the moral force of ancient Chinese teachings.

To recognize and use such material, we need to use other means of recall, beyond dreams. Impressions associated with prayer, meditation, and worship are valuable, but so are impressions received in the heat of a demanding and worthwhile task—at the previously discussed and overshadowed stages of inspiration, for example. The pain of crisis itself can trigger an altered state for recall, as can illness, orgasm, and dying. Sometimes recall can proceed well by inference—using clues from favored foods, geographical areas, primitive or foreign clothing and rites, gems, museum displays, novels and films, music, and surprising skills or language abilities. Taking a look at our antipathies and revulsions often proves more helpful than merely making up a past-life genealogy, because they illuminate our present impasses, fears, and doubts. Irrational or unlikely dislike of an individual, a racial group, a particular gender, certain animals, an occupation, an instrument of potential death, or of political and religious causes and institutions, all deserve careful inspection, and—where necessary—forgiveness and deliberate constructive engagement to reshape habitual responses that originated in the far past.

In dreams, Cayce most often called to the attention of the dreamers karmic motifs, rather than to colorful images. These themes serve many functions. They herald change (such as the initiation or resolution of a complex); pace transitions; set forth larger paths of destiny (not blind fate); support and authorize the bearing of stress; pull a theme into its parts; review gains made; and illuminate the entire growth process or some crucial part of it.

How can we recognize karmic material in dreams? The Cayce dream interpretations offer a number of clues we can use as indicators of possible karmic material in dreams. Clearly details of clothing, implements, and rites from another culture and time demand a second look; but so do variations on the scroll motif, for example, which is a symbol for destiny. Whether a document, a map, a carpet, or even a coiled dinner roll, this signal in dreams suggests attention to a multi-life design of karma. Whatever is remarkably old also deserves attention for possible karmic material in the dream, whether a relic, a site, a rite, or an ageless guide. Also deserving of attention is something intricately formed, as a jewel or crest or other artwork, for these suggest that the dream is about the soul. Cayce typically interpreted gold as soul concerns in dreams, although not all of these were associated with karma. Likewise, whatever is vastly distant from present life—whether in outer space, a distant culture, or dreaming of oneself as the other sex—requires special noting for possible karmic themes.

The content of karma is no less than our full humanity. The best clue to its presence in dreams may simply be the posing of a life theme or life riddle that we are evidently living out: the balance of yin and yang; the intertwining of wisdom and power in work; mercy and justice; ardent will and gentle grace; self-assertion and self-giving for others; and the other great biographical motifs of literature and the scriptures—all viewed under the skies of eternity. It is possible that all dreams that feel weighty to the dreamer, and incorporate a tension of opposites, may be karmic in nature. For karma is not just imported chunks from past lives; these lives continue in the present and find their ultimate meaning as subsystems in today's personhood and relationships.

Once we have used dream hints of karmic motifs, and compared dream themes with repeated waking predicaments, value conflicts, and personal growth areas, what do we do with the discoveries? Certainly we do not sulk in regret over possible past excesses or imbalances. We are in the process of hatching ourselves into larger personhood. Prying and patience, surmise and sharing, forgiveness and forging solutions—all play their parts. We are not spiritual pellets that are dropped into bodies, polished, retrieved, and dropped into new ones. The drama is surely larger and richer. Perhaps only the language of some of the mystics will suffice: it is love itself that incarnates. God seeking God.

The sufferer in personal crisis will want to approach the reincarnation hypothesis with care—not as bookkeeping of the soul, but as a blooming flower that draws on all the currents of air and earth and water, and the fire of pain, to reflect the glory of the Light in one uniquely hued soul-blossom at a time.

TRAINING TO MEET CRISES WITH GOD

According to the Cayce view, the answer to the question, "Where did God go?" is that the divine is "closer than breathing, nearer than hands and feet." He/she is intimately involved in growing us all the time, and we will want ways of keeping close to that One.

The human family has long found that certain transactions and enactments help us to come through crises successfully. These are rituals of initiation. Some initiations are appointed for turning points in the lifespan: leaving adolescence for adulthood, entering marriage, giving birth and becoming a parent, losing an intimate to death, moving into one's own expiring. Others are reserved for special tasks: setting out to battle, taking on leadership, fighting severe illness, beginning a religious or shamanic vocation, ending a marriage, or moving to a new land. Traditional cultures have often had richer social fabrics for such transitions than do our modern urban cultures, although we develop our own initiations: election rites, fraternity hazing (and that hazing by faculty called final exams), group therapy, and hospice living.

The gifted American anthropologist, Victor Turner, has studied the handling of transitions and crises, not only in his special arena of African tribes, but in historic religious groups. He reports on these crucial patterns in *The Ritual Process*. Building on the work of Arnold van Gennep about rites of passage, and using Martin Buber's distinction between I-it and I-Thou relationships,* he outlines what

*According to the philosopher Martin Buber, I-it relationships are those of partial engagement and using persons, things, or ideas. I-Thou relationships are those of total engagement in which persons, things, or ideas are allowed fully to confront or transform us.

happens in a typical ritual of transition. An individual is confronted with a great demand or a potent turning point, and is helped by the tribe or community to move from "structure" (the orderly round of daily life, with its duties, posts, schedules, ambition, service, and spiritual commitments), to "communitas" and back again.

When the time comes for a change that cuts deeply into the personhood of an individual, and therefore significantly affects the tribe or people, the need is for that special setting and grouping that Turner calls "communitas." Here the I-it transactions of daily life are subdued in favor of more awesome and psyche-transforming I-thou relationships with nature, with the arts, with charged keepers of the culture, and above all with the holy. Special procedures facilitate the change. People led into communitas are stripped of rank and treated as equals. They are dressed simply or go naked, to symbolize their common humanity; and they are addressed in relative anonymity, without titles. Gender distinctions are minimized (unless the rite is for initiation into a gender), as are those of age and wealth. Sexual activity is suspended (or made impersonal and stylized); claims of wisdom yield before seemingly foolish rites; and pride of position yields to humility.

Once communitas is established, steps are taken either to enhance the person's vital energy and focus or to turn the energy aroused by suffering into new channels. Dances, chanting, or drum beating may accompany confessions and prostrations; or the person may yield to quiet, intense concentration for hours, with only intermittent sleep. Typically use is made of nature, whether by creating an enclosure, or by introducing creatures to convey a blessing or be offered in sacrifice, or by exposure to the elements. The intent is to come to one's primal humanity, where the divine seems very near.

In this setting, ancient teachings and truths are imparted. The individual may be marked or scarred in remembrance, unless an illness or wound has already done so. Commitments and pledges to serve the larger good are sought (long ago this commitment was dramatized by human sacrifice) and made in front of the tribe, under the tutoring of elders who know the tradition and can tell awesome stories of the founders and leaders, or sacrificial efforts of the people.

The priest and shaman and helpers have their place, but initiations often seek to maximize the individual's own potency and decision-making power. For what must next happen is return to structure. The individual is not undone by the rite, but empowered and put together anew. Frequently the cycle of a complex is acted out, as the initiate is buried and resurrected in water or earth, or led into a cave or hall that signifies a womb for rebirth. Assurance must be given that trial and hardship and change are leading somewhere important, worthy of the individual's best efforts.

When it is time to reenter structure, clothing and titles are again conferred, rank and possessions once more honored, rights and duties specified. The person has been somewhere important— not only in a special location and a special time, but in the heart or soul. He or she is now expected to share that blessing with others, in the daily rounds of crafts (manufacture), barter (marketing), stockpiling (finance), leadership (management), hunting (shopping), invention (research), holy doings (worship), and family life. No initiate is expected to be just the same as before, and some even have new names or titles (as the designation Hajji after the name of a modern Muslim means that a ritual trip to Mecca or Jerusalem has been made). Yet the point of initiation is not dignity above full communal life, but enhancement of participation in that same life.

The thoughtful reader will recognize how few are the avenues in modern urban life for such alternation of structure and communitas. Falling in love is a kind of parallel (which may explain our modern absorption with romantic attachment and sexual exploits, however often these may only caricature the death and rebirth sought). Psychotherapy is another compressed version of the rite. Religious groups and movements offer their own, although these may often be so highly stylized as to rob the movement of the spirit of its renewal. Deeply felt causes can gather about them a group that develops its own rites, and celebrates its martyrs—as in the recent and ongoing Civil Rights movement. Military or revolutionary service, which strips soldiers to the role of targets, may produce times of communitas that are more than comradeship—they are rites of transformation and bonding that last a lifetime. Even heroic effort in the arts or in sports, or in medicine or the marketplace, may generate an inner rhythm of changes and imitations greater than career advancement.

Turner uses the term *liminality* (*limen* means threshold) to describe shifts below usual levels and roles and self-understandings, when the individual leaves customary patterns of daily life for temporary communitas of a transition. He warns that to remain liminal too long is to cripple one's best talents and commitments. Cults keep devotees in the liminal state, as do some therapists and some more traditional religious groupings. Ingrown leadership can be a warning sign of prolonged liminality in a group. So can the handling of normative teachings in public structure, as though they should carry the same uncritical spell they have in hushed communitas. Claims of private, self-authenticating authority (often suggested for trance counsel) warn of inappropriate liminality.

Dangers can move in the other direction, when the demands of orderly structure limit refreshing liminality to shallow rites. These dangers are familiar to those who find themselves bored by baptism, rushed through weddings, and alienated by stylized worship, dull funerals, or long-winded commencements and inaugurals. When the life-round offers little depth in genuine communitas, then only crisis can bring people together. Crisis may then be welcomed for its secret gifts, whether in enforced hospital retreats, or in military adventures, or in the intimate warfare of divorce. As Turner suggests, a fruitful social pattern keeps deep but short-term liminality close at hand, for the transitions required of us all.

Beyond the necessary alternations between liminal and nonliminal processes, Turner sees a further hope often pursued in the human family: to keep a bit of communitas, with all its wonder and humility, alive in the ordinary tasks of everyday bustle and structure. He traces that effort to keep all transactions open to bits of transformation, all players open to a center of reality beyond their own, in the history of the Franciscan order and in a Hindu sect. But he might as easily have traced it among medieval knights, Calvinist burghers, or New Age seekers, for the hunger is widespread.

Cayce's readings posed the same challenge by insisting to many that "Until you can see in each person you meet, though in error he or she may be, that which you would worship in your Lord, you haven't begun to live aright." Such glimpses of the eternal in the neighbor, or even in the enemy, are not impossible in times of deep communitas. But Cayce's counsel was not satisfied with that solution. Like Martin Buber (whose I-Thou relationship is a precise match for Cayce's demand), this source asks for incorporation of moments of open-hearted attention and awe, in all the busy scuttling about and production of results that are necessary for daily living (Buber's I-it relationships).

How did Cayce's readings propose that such a lifestyle be cultivated? They consistently paraphrased Jesus: "Inasmuch as ye do it unto the least of these, ye do it unto thy God." The readings apparently meant the stricture to be literal, for they often added, "All ye may know of thy God is what ye show, ye share, with others." Only love itself, with its taxing mix of gifts and demands, would provide the hidden secret to awaken the ultimate archetype, governing all others, which Cayce called "Christ consciousness" (not unlike what Jung denoted the Self, as the individual analogue in the psyche to the historic image of the Christ).

CHOOSING A SHARED SECRET

Anthropologists and sociologists, as well as historians of religion, have noted the pervasive hunger for a "saving secret" in a given tribe or culture. Around this secret, life-transforming fellowships can be shaped and helpful rituals for crises and transitions devised. That hunger is not lessened in our times when "saving" no longer means salvation from damnation, but more likely from manipulative commercialism and destructive militarism, or from our individual laziness and narcissism. The rituals come easily for Eskimos in an igloo, where the shaman dances with dried bones; or for Buddhists, pacing the monastery grounds with measured steps in deep absorption; or for the serene devotees of Eleusinian mysteries in ancient Greece; or for the disciplined Essenes in ancient Israel. But they come harder for us in a time where shopping malls are our de facto shrines, and passive observation is the universal television rite.

Two kinds of saving secrets preoccupy seekers, in our age as truly as elsewhere. One is the *closed secret*, reserved for initiates who have undergone a special experience and have had a higher wisdom imparted to them. (This may be seen in any gathering of Jungian or Freudian patients, in a gathering of recovering alcoholics, or among Viet Nam veterans.) The closed secret has transformative power, as Jung and others have written cogently; but it also has the limitation of excluding outsiders (even spouses and children), and the danger of ever looking backwards to decisive events and a founder's revered teachings. It may keep its advocates in liminality, rather than invite a touch of blessed grace into ordinariness.

The other kind of saving secret is the *open secret*, which centers on some life-giving process in daily existence. It is only a secret because it is too good to be believed by many, yet still capable of transformative power for those who cherish it. AA carries the seeds of such a secret or secrets by its teachings of utter dependence on a "Higher Power," restitution after wrongs done, and service of those in like predicaments. Other groups offer an open secret of love for the earth and its creatures, or a vision of a global society without nuclear threat, or family life that is wholesome and mutually empowering, or quiet growth in mystical companionship with the One.

Each such central nucleus tends to pull toward it other open secrets, which may be knit with the first. The eight steps of action to get beyond helplessness and doubt (which we described in chapter three) all carry the potential to generate variations on an open secret of cocreating with one another and the divine, even in our age of large, impersonal institutions and movements. The danger of keeping advocates in liminality is less for those who share open secrets. But, in our media age, the risk is always there of trivializing the open secret or reducing it to a closed secret for those who feel stranded and exposed in the culture by their beliefs.

Churches and synagogues and mosques, as well as Buddhist sanghas and Sufi fellowships, can turn either way—to closed or open secrets. The members may hunker down (in a worldwide movement toward fundamentalism) to defy the turbulent culture and social change by singing the old, safe songs and proclaiming the old, safe commandments. Or they may strive to break open the husk of tradition under the weight of painful and uncertain present existence, and find open and transforming wonder in what they thought were just honored traditions. Often the clash of other cultures can foster renewal of the best secret (though it may also foster defensiveness), as may be seen with the emergence of Eastern faiths in the American scene, or the rediscovery of depth in shamanism.

In the same way, alternative groupings, movements, and cults that seek to keep God close, for handling crisis and liminality and for the flow of daily doings, must choose between closed and open secrets. Many in the New Age and larger spiritual ferments of our times select a closed secret, reserving their full companionship for others who have claimed their past lives, studied their dreams, examined their auras, or can recite the chakras, sun signs, and names of spiritual rays. But others rally to a different kind of secret: the awesome goodness of the Creative Forces at an ordinary family meal and doing dishes, the glory of a child's smile, the silent sky-splash of a sunset, the peace of the dying, the prayer healing of a desperate illness, the impassioned leadership of a school board, or the delightful telepathic flash between friends. Those who have drunk long at the well marked "Cayce" have divided their responses, some going to the closed saving secret, compelling for its novelty, and some to the one that is open to all, but so lovely that one can hardly see it for its radiance.

In whatever circles the closed secret is practiced, concern for the "unfortunate" who stands outside the magic circle of believers and initiates easily disintegrates. The poor, the sick, the minorities, the lonely, the confused, the imprisoned, the betrayed, are often seen as needing enlightenment by the particular special knowledge the insiders hold. Generous efforts may be made to give them this one treasure; but binding up their wounds is messy and controversial, hardly compatible with spiritual dignity and inspiration.

Considering Cayce's life, however strange the concepts of energies and rebirth in his readings, can leave little doubt of what he chose as the guiding promise of his days. His imperative to aid the sick—to the limits of his wits and his faith and his strength, making mistakes but never giving up—was categorically central for his life and his chosen fellowships. It reflected the open love of God, which he experienced ever more deeply under the shaping winds of his tradition. Surely his care of the ill and crisis-wounded was not the only large-hearted response appropriate for a soaring vision of human destiny to be cocreators with the divine. But the person beset by severe loss may want to ask of any program or grouping that looks appealing and sounds authoritative, in times of distress, whether its gaze falls mostly inward on personal attainment by initiates, or mostly outward on those in real need.

GROWING TOWARD COMMUNITY

The art of growth through personal crises, like any other, requires the understanding of theory, such as reincarnation and karma. But the art also requires action in supportive community.

In the Cayce readings, worthwhile community is held up as normative in family life, presented as nearer to the soul's relationship with God, in its mutual vulnerability and its fresh creations, than any other grouping by itself. The readings do not devalue the single life (seriously undertaken in celibacy); but mere toying with partnership, for pleasure with limited responsibilities, is strongly discouraged in favor of marriage and family life. Yet the Cayce resource is realistic about the ever-present dangers of idolatry in family values, and the perils of those who seek to live through others, or to blame others, in relationships that misuse rather than empower intimates.

So, right alongside family covenants, the Cayce resource presents those formal and informal bondings that temper and enlarge households, clans, and tribes. Chief among these are the great spiritual communities, accountable to rich traditions. But, in the Cayce view, historic spiritual groupings are sterile if they do not spill out into community-making in many of life's arenas (as his life-readings show in the best of incarnations lived in many cultures). The central secrets, the rhythms of liminality, the dance of attunement with service—all can be found in business firms, in orchestras, in athletic teams, in political protest movements, on campuses, or anywhere else that a cocreating lifestyle calls forth organization that has a center transparent to the divine, however it is named or unnamed.

On the other hand, just keeping busy in many hopeful and helpful groupings does not suffice for the nurture of precious archetypes, which are the nucleus of serious growth and innovation. In this view, the peril of many moderns who abandon historic spiritual traditions is inner drying up of the springs of new life. To facilitate claiming the great themes of human existence, the Cayce readings suggest in detail the use of small, leaderless search-and-study groups that are strongly but not narrowly tipped to communitas. In these, each process in scripture or myth can be matched with tonight's dreams and tomorrow's journal entries, as well as shared with committed companions.

Some of Cayce's friends, drawing on his readings, developed two anonymous (note well the anonymity) devotional and growth manuals, filled with their own personal but disciplined reflections and experiences. The manuals, entitled *A Search for God*, Books I and II, have been used in thousands of small groups that now reach around the world. They are not offered as the last word on anything. (In fact the introduction to these books, which are a kind of repeatable course, includes a delightful sentence that points to open secrets: "There is nothing new here.") Accompanied by group-chosen disciplines and daily prayer for each member, these manuals embody the kind of sequence in spiritual growth that can make grown-ups out of today's hungry offspring of media stimulation.

A full picture of the Cayce resource on community can help those who have been buffeted by crisis, or who just want a more lovely and lovable existence. Such communities can be small gatherings of companions of the way, who meet weekly to explore life's big issues in disciplined adventures; and larger congregations and institutions, which offer engagements across age levels and social classes, rich corporate worship, potent historic concepts, vital activities of social service and social change, and daring cooperation beyond the local level. Each type of effort, small and large, stretches and renews the other, moving together, in a modern pilgrimage that includes both communitas and structure, toward a world that can be—in Martin Buber's phrase—"community all through."

PART II

The Practice of Growing Through Personal Crisis

7

There Is Always
a Way to Begin

THE ART OF GROWING through personal crisis requires us to unroll some large maps, and to explore new terrain for weeks or even months. We need theories, models, and sequences, such as we have examined in previous chapters. Taking on a particular crisis bursts with definite demands: *right now*. We have to choose what to say on the phone, whom to invite over, when to weep and when to be brave, when to rest and when to get busy, when to get advice and when to go apart for prayer, what to change at once and what to put off for reflection. The practice of growing through personal crisis shouts at us: put first things first!

STRATEGIES FOR GROWTH

To grow through personal crisis, we need definite strategies. Let us take a look at some strategies we can hold on to as we walk from the darkness to the Light.

1. Begin with Trust

In the view of the Cayce resource, there is always a way to begin. Something will be close at hand that we can grab and hold tight, even when our world spins out of control and we feel terribly alone and vulnerable, guilty and anxious. That something is trust—trust in God's presence and caring, trust in God's aid, trust in God's ability to pull forth strength and wisdom and even loveliness from such difficult times.

This trust is not blind resignation, nor collapse into childish helplessness. It is reaching out to explore, to engage, to grow, and to learn. To find someone there, we have to risk crying out to the unseen; we have to make a huge surmise, and patiently watch what comes of it, tired and rattled as we may be. For "he that seeks the Lord must believe that He is," as the Cayce resource points out. Otherwise "doubting has already builded that barrier that prevents the proper understanding, whether as to physical, mental, or spiritual attributes, or spiritual aid, or mental aid, or physical aid." This trust does not require us to understand all about God, agree to creeds, or undertake elaborate rituals. It asks for an open heart, a willing spirit, and some definite activities in the midst of paralyzing crisis.

No single claim in the Cayce readings is more central than the promise that God will meet us: right where we are, in our flesh and our consciousness, in our badgered circumstances. Over and over this counsel insists that our bodies are "the temples of the living God," where true communing can and will take place, if we seek it. We need not travel to a fabled holy city, nor enter a vaulted cathedral, nor seek out a spiritual master. We need not wait until we die, nor wait for ecstasy to seize us on a mountaintop. Right now, closer than the telephone, quicker than the next breath, the One draws near to us, with definite guidance, definite strength, definite assurance of whom we touch.

Pain splits us open to this reality. We may have doubted, dodged, and delayed the encounter for years. Or we may have protested our faith and our trust, yet half-consciously hedged, sought other insurance for bad times, collected other comfort. Suffering ignores all this, and goes right to work opening channels in the body and the mind, firing up chakras, unwrapping invisible archetypes. All we have to do is reach out, a little more and a little more.

We must also become quiet. "Turn within" is the steady counsel of the readings. This does not mean that we should rely on our own memories, our own skills, our own favorite sayings—although these may help. The turning within is most of all to receive gifts that are delivered there: the presence of the divine, and its assurances that the universe is quietly on our side.

More often than not, the people who turned to Cayce for guidance did so in trying times. His responses were consistent. When asked, "Is there any way I can handle better the daily situations which become more difficult?" he replied, "Turn more *within* for those answers. Not to segregate nor separate self from the problems nor from the activities. But *know* and experience that the answer to this or that problem comes most from within self" (no. 1023–2).*

To another Cayce explained, "For, as He has given (which is the greater promise from the foundation of the world) 'If ye call, I will hear, and answer speedily—though ye be far away, I will hear—I will answer.' That is the attitude that the self shall hold towards those problems where there are disputes, discouragings, disappointments. Yea, they often arise in the experience of all." Cayce speaks of this promise as the most significant since the beginning of creation. Yet to the same person he also mentions God's patient nurturance, in which trials and blows are not random, but embedded in the soul's journey of growth through many lives. "But think, O Child, how oft thou must have disappointed thy Maker, when He hath given thee the opportunity and calls, 'The day of the Lord is at hand,' [as] to all of those who will hear His voice" (no. 1747–5).

The promise of being met right where we are is not a promise of blinding flashes, or of voices speaking loudly in the head. It is not one of being taken over by spiritual guides or invaded by higher forces. It is a promise of little promptings and nudges, of tips to one side or another in a choice, of urgings to make the truly helpful response, of

*Each of the Edgar Cayce readings has been assigned a two-part number to provide easy reference. Each person who received a reading was given an anonymous number; this is the first half of the two-part number. Since many individuals obtained more than one reading, the second number designates the number of that reading in the series. Reading no. 1023–2 was given for a person who was assigned case number 1023. This particular reading was the second one this person obtained from Cayce.

assurance that we are not alone and never were. In time, such aid may extend to complete plans, entire outlines, whole campaigns, as we have seen in tracing the anatomy of inspiration. But the beginning is just little bits of meaning and direction that tug at us when we make time to step aside and wait on the One, who knows us better than we know ourselves, and who cares with unflagging delight that we step forth on our best.

The Cayce resource does not reserve the promise of God's love and guidance to quiet times. His readings also invite people to discover how intimately God meets us and suffers with us in action.

> Meet the Father face to face through patience with self and others, seeing in those that would speak evil of thee, those that would despitefully use thee, those even who would take advantage of thy gentleness, thy kindness, only the good . . . [Do it] knowing that none may do such save that the power is given them through the Giver of *all* power, *all* life, that thou — through thine own experience — may know that the Father suffereth with each child He has purged, that it may be a companion with Him. (no. 695–1)

The Cayce readings speak of a God who suffers intimately and deeply with each of us now, as we meet the difficult circumstances that stretch us to our full stature. Even when it seems that hardship and loss will undo us, the promise is of a steadying hand, appointing all things and restraining them, in the journeys of our days.

2. What We Need Is Available

The first assurance we need to trust, as a perspective for beginning on each crisis, is that God will meet us, right where we are. The next is that all the resources we need are at hand, both within us and around us. Archetypes are ready to shape our skills, focus our vision, transmute our values. The Cayce readings insist about such crucial resources that "The *body* is a pattern, it is an ensample [*sic*] of all the forces of the universe itself" (no. 2153–6); and " . . . the soul of man, thy soul, encompasses *all* in this solar system or others" (no. 5755–2).

What we need really can occur to us, and grow into our very muscles and nerves, for action. And these same archetypes will draw from the universe around us the opportunities and assets that crisis requires, as "Like attracts like." The great central process of creating solutions from resources at hand shines in the often-cited phrase in the Cayce readings: "The Spirit is the life, mind is the builder, and the physical is the result." Our first choice is to make certain that what we seek is worthy of being called "the Spirit." Is it vital, noble, and generous, informed by grace and truth? If so, we can take up the outcomes fitting to that Spirit, plan with them, study their parts and stages, as we make our minds architects of a richer reality. What follows—sooner or later, but always on track—is the "physical" consequences in our bodies, our settings, our opportunities, our relationships.

3. We Have a Large Destiny

We each have a tremendous destiny, within which we can make permanent gains. Frustrations, betrayals, losses can be put into a larger scheme, as we grow into the awareness that we are living souls, not just victims of social forces and childhood conditioning. Trying to see our own biographies across thousands of years is no snap. But wrestling with that possibility can take away panic, when affairs go badly. According to Cayce, it is always fear that cripples us most. No single attitude or emotion does us more damage. So we need to get our heads up and look for the stars; only they are old enough to remind us of our size and destiny in the dance of creation.

Now comes the affirmation that suffering is purposeful within this destiny, if we choose it to be. Crises arrive not to humiliate us before a divine potentate, but to light our way by flames of fire, toward specific directions where we need to grow. "Do not attempt to go around the Cross" is the Cayce counsel, sobering but not harsh. For the cross that is meant here is not senseless killing, but steady refinement of our beings. The idea is not that we grow only through peril and suffering—far from it. We grow as cocreators with the ever-flowing Source every time we play with a child, create a tune, manage a sales campaign, clean up toxic wastes. But we also grow through suffering, which is God's left-handed blessing.

Not surprisingly, Cayce's readings observe that those who seek to grow the most will initially suffer the most, as the purging and refining of all that is precious in us gets speeded up a bit. But when we swim through heavy surf, walk through no-man's land, slide onto the surgical table, tumble down cliffs of rejection, the promise is that we can make permanent gains in the fruits of the spirit: patience, goodwill, truthfulness, justice, inventiveness—all such fuller humanness as may make God smile along with our own surprised grins.

4. Risk Being Constructive

In tough times, we must not blame others, but be constructive in our responses—even if "it takes the hide off." None of us gets away without temptation to saddle others with our misfortunes: neglectful parents, ungrateful bosses, hasty doctors, troublesome offspring, mean peers. But the counsel in the Cayce readings is to "magnify the agreements, minimize the disagreements," recognizing that we may understand little of where the other person stands. If we attack and belittle others, the pettiness creeps into our own souls and shrinks them.

Often Cayce's counsel used pithy sayings to make the point. "Better to trust one soul, and that deceiving, than to doubt that one, in whom believing, would have blessed thy life with truer meaning." Faced with abuse or betrayal, such an approach takes all our wills. Yet trying it, not alone but with God's company—and "one with God is a great majority"—can often free us from petrifying doubt of our own adequacy. To smile, to speak gently of others' shortcomings, to pick out something worthwhile in a general mess—these steps set loose in our veins a nectar that is hard to describe, but harder still to give up, because it is rich love in action. The point of sharing in small search-and-support groups is often to cultivate precisely these responses.

5. Seek Definite Guidance

When we begin with such perspectives and strategies, the Cayce readings offer the assurance that we can get definite guidance in even the most tangled distresses. They pick out the capacity of the unconscious (widely noted by diviners in many cultures, but also by the faithful who need no consulting apparatus) to respond to yes-or-no choices, even when the issues are complex and require the unconscious to put together many pieces into an intuitive whole.

> Prayer and meditation, to be sure . . . [then] in thine own mind, decide as to whether this or that direction is right. Then pray on it, and leave it alone. Then suddenly ye will have the answer, yes or no. Then with that Yes or No, take it again to Him in prayer, "Show me the way." And Yes or No will again direct thee from deep within. (no. 3250–1)

This seemingly simple process is actually quite sophisticated. It requires us first to use consciousness as far as we can take it in a difficult situation, weighing alternatives. Tired as we may be, we must analyze the problem, try out approaches, consider modifying forces, develop alternative scenarios. But it is also essential to go back to primary values, specifying the ideals we have chosen to govern behavior. Just spinning off possibilities will not do; we need to weigh the options in the scales of our best aspirations, even if we must name these afresh.

Then we must sort through the alternatives and choose the one that looks and feels best, even if it is the best of a sorry lot, or costly to our fortitude or patience to carry out. It should be practical and workable (as far as we can guess), yet have a ring of potential quality and proportion. Often we need to try explaining our chosen solution to some trusted intimates—not just for their approval, but to see for ourselves whether we are making sense. We may well test our plan against norms of scripture or biography that we cherish. Now we set forth the choice; we may write it out if we need that step to get clear, or say it to ourselves in our heads.

Next prayer and meditation, as well as corporate worship, enter the process in a decisive way. We step close to the divine—not for favors, but for true companionship and unselfish creativity. In that context, after the heart is warmed and the senses stilled, we set before God the choice we have made, in yes or no form. Note that this is not a general cry for help (although that, too, has its place, when we are initially too distraught to seek such definite guidance). It is a specific proposal in a form that the unconscious can readily process, under the winds of the Spirit. Yes or no?

As Cayce suggests, with this kind of preparation, an initial response may come in minutes (though often it takes hours). Meantime, leaving it alone means not pushing or stewing, but just incubating—waiting, turning to something else, or sleeping on it. The prompting will appear. If the response is no—whether the whole approach is faulty, or just some feature—we go back to the drawing board and work up another proposal that can win a yes-or-no reply. If the response is yes, we do not leap into action, unless emergency dictates. Instead we bring the proposal back for further validation, not in doubt, but in respect for the seriousness of the guidance process. When it is confirmed again, and keeps its steady quality in our consciousness, then we act on it and remember to give thanks for the guidance.

In the Cayce view, this kind of procedure is offered for predicaments as varied as deciding on surgery, discriminating among job offers, choosing between suitors, or planning how to resolve a quarrel. It is not the only way to solve problems (as we have indicated in discussing the larger movement of energies in inspiration). But it is a resource always available in times of distress, just as it is for sorting out options when we are not troubled, but only want the best outcome among several. It is predicated on the assumption that God will meet us in our own consciousness, using all the natural resources of the psyche, including wide-ranging ESP and forgotten treasures learned in one's long soul journey.

WHAT WE MAY EXPECT

What will be the outcome of using these strategies? We may expect not only to begin resolving the baffling riddles of our activities, but to grow Godward. Walking in the companionship that does not fail, we change, until both we and others notice that something prized is growing in us, day by day. "So live," Cayce's readings advised in a simple but potent formula, "that others will be glad to see thee come, sorry to see thee go."

As to the specific qualities that may emerge from a life pledged to meet hardship with the One, we can trust that we are fashioned to glorify God from our own uniqueness. "Who can tell a rose to be beautiful?" Cayce's readings often asked. "Who can tell the wind how to blow, who can tell the sun how to shine, who can tell a baby how to smile?" Each soul comes equipped, snowflake-like, with its own unique pattern for growth.

Three kinds of crises lend themselves to using these strategies: crises of the heart, crises of work and social problems, and crises of colliding with ourselves. We will turn to these now.

8

Crises of the Heart

FEW KINDS OF PAIN hurt as much as damage to a cherished relationship. When the heart breaks with such a loss, it seems to affect every aspect of our lives. Whether the blow be death, divorce, desertion, serious illness of a beloved, or breakdown of familiar patterns of intimacy, the ripples reach all through our world. Often we must move to a new location, find new friends, change our income and living standards, enter new schools. We take on new debts, find we are sleeping, eating, and dressing differently, revise our play, and barely recognize holiday celebrations we thought would never change.

DEATH

Death heads the list of shocks. The worst, by general consensus, is the death of a spouse, lover, although death of a child has an unthinkable arbitrariness all its own. The suicide of someone close to us not only brings grief, but often fright—we wonder if we, too, might break.

The death of a loved friend or relative can disorient us, because one of the people we live by (as seen in their place in our dreams) is not there to draw us out, to need us, to challenge us, to bless us, to define us. If the person who died is someone we truly loved, we find that we are permanently changed. There is a cavity in our beings that cannot be filled, although time may dull its pain. But the wise know that death not only robs us, it redesigns us, even as it confers on us the robes of initiation into a universal transition that can transfigure the soul.

Elisabeth Kübler-Ross and others have traced familiar steps in the dying process: denial, anger, bargaining, depression, and finally acceptance. Each has its counterpart for the mourner. No step is easy, for each feels overwhelming in its season. Let's take a look at fresh approaches offered by the Cayce resource, which we can use to seek a beginning with death's crisis of the heart.

The Cayce readings do not minimize grief. Some of their tenderest passages are for those whose lives have been ripped apart by death, especially the untimely death of the young or those in the prime of their days. The readings counsel rest, moderate activity, little or no medication, the company of wise and gentle associates, and much patience, as well as time spent in nature. Yet right beside the grieving they place the firm assurance that like birth, death is only a transition, a passage through "God's other door." The intent is not to minimize the devastating upheavals that death brings into our lives. It is rather to take away the panic we feel because this unique relationship is over.

Most of us sense, correctly, that when we lose someone dear we lose a chunk of ourselves. If the universe is designed to let these pieces just disappear forever, then we are each built to fall apart, however long and bravely we may put off the collapse. Typically, the Cayce readings do not ask that mourners take the reality of life after death on blind faith, but invite sufferers to explore it. They do not, however, encourage seeking communication with the dead through mediums, or through automatic writing or Ouija boards. Instead they point out that using any kind of automatism leaves the wounded survivor open to invasion or disturbance by troubled souls on the other side of death, who seek expression through the living because they cannot bear to move on in their appointed paths. Nor do the readings encourage the living to get guidance and advice from the dead: the dead are not likely to be any wiser by the sheer event of expiring than they were while among us! We already have enough temptations to dependency in our lives, without adding dependency on messages from the disembodied. Yet they affirm that love is meant to reach beyond the grave, and that experience of the not-so-dead whom we cherish is freely allowed in God's mercy, though not frequently enough to entrap the bereaved.

The Cayce counsel warns that the state after this life is so different that it cannot be grasped by ordinary consciousness and reasoning. It just slips out of comprehension, like trying to catch one's shadow in the hand. But when consciousness alters—whether in sleep, in prayer, in vision, or in pain—then it may momentarily align itself with the reality of after-death existence to allow love to touch the beloved. Over and over again Cayce pointed out to seekers that their dreams of those parted from them were capable of tempering great doubts about the reality of life and growth beyond death. In our counseling, we have used these ideas and added our own experiences, to help scores of death-wounded people find their way to memorable dream contacts.

Although one might expect such dreams to be overwhelmingly emotional, they are not; the feelings are typically gentle, wondering, joyous, and full of thanksigving. What matters is assurance that the one who has gone on is truly and fully alive, and continues loving. Just a touch will suffice for an entire embrace, for the dreamer is immensely sensitive in such encounters. Exchanged glances of infinite caring will do. Wakening, the dreamer wonders why more was not said, and why explanations were not given as to various mysteries of after-death states. But the purpose of such dreams seems to be communion, not communication—of information we could not use, in any case.

Several features distinguish such dreams from those in which the beloved appears as a memory, or as a symbol of unique qualities (both also significant dream functions). In the dreams that step right through the doorway of death, soft light often suffuses the scene. We see the people on the next plane as they looked at their optimum age—no longer ill or aged, but whole and vital. Seeing this healthfulness often profoundly touches the dreamer, since love ever longs for the best in the other. Gestures and phrases may be exchanged to seal the reality of the encounter, and token objects may be used to recall the bonds celebrated—a watch, a garment, a musical instrument, a book. The scene may shift to a mutually loved outdoor setting. If music accompanies the light, it will be as gentle as a flute or a child's song, not a crashing symphony. Often there are smiles, rarely tears; for thanksgiving is in the air, blessing all past memories and all future hopes of reunion and greater creations together.

Sometimes, however, the person we meet is sad, disconsolate, or confused. Not infrequently, in the Cayce readings, this is the initial state of those who have impulsively committed suicide, or overdosed on drugs. The Cayce injunction follows (as it does about all who have died) to pray for them, just as earnestly as when they were on this plane. Prayer, in this view, helps to create a light and focus that leads the newly dead person to helpers and new growth on the next plane. Here the Cayce materials support a position taken by Roman Catholic and Episcopal traditions. In contrast, much of Protestant faith has assumed that death confers immediate access to the fullness of the divine—when it adopts any view of the process at all. Instead, the Cayce viewpoint suggests that loving prayer can be helpful for weeks or months after a death. Prayer can also be helpful at anniversaries or on special occasions, when a gentle inward prompting suggests that the departed have not gone anywhere, except in consciousness. At the same time, such prayer must not become a vehicle for clinging to the one who has gone through death's doorway, because it can hold the soul back from its appointed growth. The prayer of blessing is appropriate, as Jews know about the mourner's year of saying *kaddish*. Dreamers report that even the newborn or infants appear in such dreams, smiling or giving recognition of the renewed relationship. The impact on distraught parents can be memorable, as we have often seen in our work.

Do those who love us continue to watch out for us, encourage us, warn us, and pray for us in turn? Such dreams suggest that they do. The same assurance comes from moments in prayer or other heightened states, when the presence of those gone on is as real as the presence of the living. This presence may be brief—perhaps lasting an hour or a day—but it can get us through the worst of a crisis. In the Cayce view, also supported in such dreams, the soul that has traveled through death moves increasingly into new orbits of awareness and growth, from which it may dip back into our lives, yet still keep its forward motion.

Are these souls in some sort of heaven or hell? According to the Cayce readings, the individual's own unconscious—especially the subconscious (what Jung would call the personal unconscious)—supplies the outlines of the after-death state, where the subconscious becomes consciousness. We become next, and we experience there, just who we have been here—not more and not less, until we start growing again in the many mansions appointed for existence beyond earth's plane.

How shall we know when to expect a meeting or blessing from those we so gravely miss? In the Cayce view, the soul often needs a period of rest and reorientation after the body dies. This may take a few weeks or longer. During this time, contact is unlikely, although it can happen to the living who are especially sensitive to such impressions. It is not unheard of for mourners to "see" the dead sharing in their own funerals, relishing the friends and relatives who have gathered, as well as celebrating all that has been shared.

The general rule in the Cayce readings appears to be this: meet the dead in the One. Put the trust in the ultimate reality to know when to open the gates of perception. Then enter the relationship with appreciation, not demands for wonders or satisfaction of curiosity. The spirit of this trust should also guide the telling of the experience of encounter. For not all will understand, and some will even belittle what can be as precious as any kiss or promise, from those who once walked and ate and slept and argued and wept beside us.

ALIENATION AND DIVORCE

The human family has ceremonies to untie the knots that death loosens, but it is not so well equipped to untie the knots of marriage, or the ties between lovers. Even so, divorce or separation bring their own loneliness and grief. Parting in our society is often loaded with regret, blame, and unfinished business, so turbulent as to shut out any but partisan friends and relatives. Sometimes the pain is so great that the partners just freeze each other into stiff images to be manipulated, but not engaged.

The Cayce readings offer some guidelines about separation that are not common in our culture. Using the long perspective of soul growth in reincarnation, the readings affirm that monogamous marriage is the appointed path for the fullest gain of most souls—although celibacy has its place for some. These readings don't pull any punches. They ask each individual to make a choice between an ideal of marriage or an ideal of the single life for this incarnation, and then hold to it. Those who profess one ideal and act counter to it only tangle up their own souls and set the stage for constricting karma. The readings do not encourage premarital sex, and almost uniformly discourage extramarital sex, on the principle that vows should be taken seriously or not taken at all. However, the final choices in each situation are left to each individual to make, in communion with the divine. The intent is not to fit people to arbitrary rules, but to their own best chosen purposes; for morality here is more a matter of the heart than of outward actions alone.

In an interesting use of scriptural images, the readings affirm, "All love is lawful, but not all is expedient unto good works." The concept is that real love—cherishing the other person in a relationship committed to mutual growth—is the essence of cocreating. It therefore carries its own validation, whether in or out of marriage, and presumably in homosexuality (though not in incest, which collapses the tension in relationships necessary for real growth). Yet the fruition of such love, by its very nature, is such "good works" as bearing children, building social structures and families, keeping promises. These, too, are of the essence of cocreating. They modify and shape the promise primal attraction and mutuality afford. Each soul is given freedom to plumb dimensions of tender commitments, and must make its own choices. Cayce pointed out principles and consequences, but he typically handed the issues to the person to decide.

What then of that special kind of crisis that comes with falling out of love, or falling in love outside of vows? As might be expected, the Cayce readings do not rest relationships as heavily on emotions as on ideals. Rather than falling into or out of love, we should seek to grow in love, learning to share and to encourage and to celebrate one another. Part of this growing is ever forgiving—for who does not fall short? In the Cayce view, marital infidelity is not sufficient grounds for separation or divorce. Generally, it can and should be forgiven and grown past, within the vows taken before God.

Behavior that can legitimately lead to divorce consists of such continuous cruelty or neglect or belittling by one partner that the other loses the opportunity for soul growth. The Cayce readings do not apply this standard lightly, or leave it to the whims of an individual's pleasure and self-justification. But when children are abused and their lives distorted, dissolution of a family may become necessary. The same principle applies to misuse of opportunities with a partner. Still, the Cayce counsel urged people over and over again to strive to work out their differences, putting the other person's legitimate needs to the fore, because—in the worldview of reincarnation—what couples do not accomplish now they will be likely to address again, whether with the same partner or another. Better to do it now, and move on to larger destinies, was the counsel.

According to Cayce, similar principles apply to other endings in intimate relationships, such as struggles for custody of children. Here the needs of the children, as gifts of the Creator, are given strong priority, though not exclusive consideration. In the Cayce perspective, each child born to a couple is in some sense a seal of viability and hope given to the relationship. Humans exercise conception, but only God determines whether a living soul enters the body. So breaking up a family carries serious consequences, in this view, although God will work with any solution couples seek in full gravity. The divine seeks to bring forth the best for each family member, although the road might require the karma of experiencing in turn what one arbitrarily rejects in a partner.

Separation is not usually encouraged by the Cayce readings as an inadequate solution, unless basic welfare is endangered. But this does not mean that mere physical closeness qualifies as married love. Arguments and criticism can tear apart a marriage, while keeping it housed in one building; as can selfish denial or abuse of sexual sharing—that encounter of the flesh that the readings saw as natural as the falling of snow in winter, not as a trap.

FAMILY CHANGES

Not all family crises are marital, of course. Some individuals experience crisis because they have *not* found a partner in loving. (Although the surprising assertion appears in the readings that everyone who truly wants a mate, and is willing to take the required risks, will find one in the mercies of God.)

The readings present family life as the highest of human callings—not at the expense of daily work, but as a counterpoint and fruition for it, so that "those who shun same will have much to answer for." In this view, the deep relationships of the household, not necessarily of marriage, are enactments of the soul opening itself to God.

Adoption of children into the family circle found welcome support in the Cayce view of reincarnation—where, in a sense, all new souls are adopted, or may be said to adopt their families at birth. What matters in this perspective is far less the biology of procreation than the psychology of cocreation, which shapes each step of the family's journey together. In the Cayce view, one does not simply rear the young, from some superior adult position. One loves and is vulnerable to the young, in the same mysterious movement of the spirit that guides all real caring. In the next life, one may *be* the young, with a present child as parent or spouse. All roles are relativized in such a perspective, though not obliterated, just as are differences of gender. How we treat our intimate friends and relatives determines whether we shall have free choice for growth in another round of birth, or the need to endure what we despised or misused in someone's flesh or selfhood or temperament within the present family unit. Such perspectives may temper many a strident family crisis, and turn eyes to far horizons of unknown adventures together.

Not surprisingly, the "empty nest" problem for parents is addressed soberly. Parents are encouraged to plan ahead for the necessary exit of children, through alternate avenues for the vital energies originally called forth by the adventures of making a home.

The readings offer a perspective of strong preference to child rearing as a full vocation, and suggest that only a minority of parents can fruitfully undertake both the home and a career side by side—although those whose talents and karma supported it were firmly encouraged. In Cayce's time, of course, the wife generally did not work outside the home while the children were young, although today this is true for more than half of contemporary American families. Many of the heartbreaking crises in today's families revolve around these issues. Our culture does not accept the Cayce picture of rearing children as a full vocation, if it requires a lowered standard of living.

For these painful questions, often the basis for tears and rage in modern marriages, only the steps we have outlined for securing shared guidance will suffice, not rules or customs alone. As so often in human experience, freedom brings with it new challenges and threats, but also new potentials for growth.

ABUSE AND NEGLECT

Violence or willful assertion can destroy the bonds of marriage and family, and cripple or destroy the players. The element of cruelty heightens all stresses, sometimes beyond enduring—partly because it carries an aspect of choice, which exacerbates the wounds of loss by turning them into betrayal and abuse. The violence may be the cold cruelty of neglect and desertion; the whiplash impacts of alcoholism and drug abuse; or the heated violations in beatings, rape, incest, or custody kidnappings. All carry the extra force of creating in the victims profound rage and self-doubt, upsetting them for years or even lifetimes.

The challenge is to engage the outrage responsibly, to restore self-respect and sanity to those who are victimized. There is no reason, in the Cayce perspective, to expect that once powerful emotions are unleashed in victims, they can simply be dropped, or amputated by professional intervention. They can only be redirected, as when chronic anger is turned into boldness and humor, or self-pity into genuine compassion. For this purpose, the Cayce picture of chakras or centers is a challenge to adult growth. The centers, which can be destructive if allowed indulgent and vengeful expression, can also become the individual's greatest strength—if their quality is redirected, while their force remains.

Not everyone finds the concept of reincarnation helpful when intimacy is shattered by abuse or neglect. Yet for those able to work with it, the suggestion is at times offered in readings that their own souls have also tasted the thrill of rejecting, exiling, hurting, or manipulating, and can now learn a lasting and constructive lesson. In our psychotherapy practice, we have often noted that what individuals dread most is that which they know they could also do to others. Only when they find that they will not hurt those vulnerable to them, however justified the circumstances, can they finally put down the panic that brutalizing engenders.

EMOTIONAL DEMANDS

Need and responsibility can threaten to overwhelm us, making staggering demands on our energy, patience, creativity—and on our love. Chronic physical or mental illness of someone close heads the list. As long as the illness continues, some part of us is gone away, to stay at the bedside or the heartside of the afflicted person who is part of us. We may eat, play, work, make love, and even travel. But nothing changes the situation; some part of our deep consciousness is pledged to the sufferer and keeps vigil there.

When illness or injury comes swiftly, we often receive hearty support from relatives, friends, coworkers, and companions in faith, who know from their own experience what we must be undergoing. But when the illness drags on, or injury turns into permanent crippling, people forget to express the same compassion. We are left alone in tears and anxiety, or helpless rage.

In the Cayce view, such trials come to the entire family, not just to the person who is ill or injured. They come as opportunities, not as retribution for past excesses. To be sure, some or all of the souls in the family unit may be encountering karma, in which the soul has to compare the far—yet never absent—past with the present distress. But nobody is allowed simply to patronize the primary sufferer. In the Cayce view, some souls undertake exceptional hardship on behalf of an entire family, all of whom must have the opportunity to grow through the heavy demands of the persistent suffering. The resources of a merciful God are needed here—from professional assistance to the steady prayers and encouragement of a larger circle. The seriously ill individual has a special opportunity, which the Cayce readings spelled out again and again, to be a light to others with whatever can be mustered of smiles, gratitude, fortitude, and humor.

Something that seems to participants like the thrust of whole life-times can be lived out in a few months of cancer or AIDS or injuries from burns or auto accidents, or in the longer torment of schizophrenia or depression. Every human goodness is magnified by the ambient pain, but so is carelessness or neglect—unless the pain is brought to the very thrones of grace by persistent prayer and consistent service and goodwill. Divorce and desertion, rape and violence, each have their dramatic side, which turns them into social rituals, for better or worse. But numbing failure of the body or mind within the family circle leaves outsiders threatened. They wonder whether they might be so visited, and doubt that they could provide the un-stinting caregiving—so that they almost envy the providers for their evident stature of soul, yet find themselves uncertain how to speak about it. The rituals of aid for prolonged illness and injury are few and awkward, in our culture. Fortunately, the use of small groups, whose participants share similar predicaments of trial and loss, is growing into what is today called a "recovery movement" in AA circles and elsewhere.

When the illness is addiction, social support is often difficult to come by, for the affliction carries moral overtones. Cayce counseled family and friends of such addicts to "pray like the devil," in the evident conviction that inner reinforcement could tip the balance when outside pressures—necessary pressures—might not. His readings seemed aware of the subtle collusion in families, so that spouses of addicts are victims of themselves and their feelings of helplessness.

He urged relatives to find their own ideals and stick to them. Linking prayer to cure or relief from addiction brought Cayce close to Jung, who observed (in a famous letter to an AA member) that the answer had to be "Spiritus contra spiritum." Only the living Spirit is strong and deep enough to cure the love of bottled spirits and their artificial ecstasies, close enough to the real thing to beguile many. Small groups, however, as AA has demonstrated, can be immensely potent for dealing with the crises of addiction, including drug abuse, eating, and gambling.

The extraordinary and sometimes lifelong demands of the handicapped and retarded came up many times in Cayce readings. Again, the focus was on opportunity for the entire family. As a consequence, parents were usually advised not simply to put away a severely retarded child, but to make a place for it in the family circle, as a soul that had chosen this household and these people for the special growth of all involved. To be sure, the needs of other children were not ignored, and various kinds of solutions were offered, depending on age levels. The capacity for tender, unfeigned loving and joy, so often reported about retarded children, came under Cayce's scrutiny as evidence that the soul was in its self-chosen bonds. Here, too, the readings counseled prayer, but with a difference that has proved important in many families.

Cayce advised the parent to offer not only prayer, but constructive suggestions out loud as the child falls asleep—repeatedly picturing his or her capacities and attitudes. In our experience, this has proved to be just as rewarding as Cayce predicted. Parents need to be the agents of such bedtime suggestion. Recordings, professionals, or hired substitutes will not work, because personal love is part of the cure. But in the decades since Cayce first spelled out this place to begin for helping the special child, many a child has exceeded the supposed limits of its training or education or self-care.

UNWANTED INTIMACY

Unwanted intimacy or dependence can also create crises of the heart. Aged or poverty-stricken relatives may have to move in with us, creating havoc in our routines. Few are prepared for the upheaval of new rituals of meals and bathrooms and quiet times, or for the added economic burdens and constrictions of space and privacy. But the privilege of sponsoring a soul can be a sweeping journey to mutual stature. The call for compassion is heightened when the one forced to enter the family circle is an elderly parent, because the offspring inspect every flaw as a sign of their destiny. This situation presents opportunities for learning that the greatest spiritual gift may not be wondrous visions or healings or writings, but the delicate art of shutting the mouth in timely fashion.

The problem of invasion of the family circle is reversed, and no easier, if it becomes necessary to put an aging relative in a nursing home. Grown men and women shrink before this task, which seems so thankless when one recalls the loving care the aged person freely gave us decades ago. Cayce was not quick to recommend this solution; yet in our culture, which lacks extended family housing compounds (as compared with many traditional or "primitive" societies), it may come as yet another crisis for love—to be followed by riddles of how to handle endless visits that should not become perfunctory, but often do.

Less obvious are the strains on family rhythms when one member tries to live through another. Whether a parent living through children, or a spouse living through a mate, the violations of selfhood are exhausting, demeaning, and infectious. There is already enough incestuous collusion under the surface in any marriage or family. It comes from that part of each of us which fights against independence and responsibility in the hope that life can be bought more cheaply. When crippling dependence is acted out, there is hell to pay. It erupts not only in quarrels and infidelity, but even in illness, as the living spirit strikes out against the patterns.

Living your life through a child, which infects it with both grandeur and despair, is not the only way to torture the young. Over and over Cayce warned, "Don't break the spirit." His readings were not hesitant to advise limits, but insisted that with every precept there must go consistent example, or else "What you are speaks so loud that others can't hear what you say." Encouragement needs to outweigh criticism, appreciation outrank punishment, and giving of self exceed mere manipulation of possessions and privileges. Not surprisingly, Cayce saw the soul of an adult mirrored in what it offered to children, or in what it withheld.

But children also present parents with crises when they must claim their freedom by turning to peers, lest they be bound to their elders for a lifetime. Parents find, as Jung pointed out, that whatever they fail to live out, their children are now obsessed with—sex, money, education, power, religion. Partly the children use these as weapons against the gods—which their powerful parents are. But at a deeper level, they pick up the hidden ambiguity, the secret doubts and fears of their elders, and then parade around these fascinating idols that so frightened their parents.

As if adolescent causes, emotions, and rebellions were not enough, some parents find themselves having to push their children out of the nest. Parents who are not secure in their own identities cannot do this well. They become alternately punitive and protective, in a rhythm the young person learns how to play upon only too easily. Happy are the parents who find a non-family adult to sponsor one or more of their youths. This is warmly encouraged in the Cayce readings, both for the young people trying to find their ways and for the sponsors themselves.

9

Crises of Work
and Social Problems

Our culture consumes crises in its incessant television and film fare. Crises of our labors fall all too easily into melodrama, pitting the good guys against the bad guys, even though we all know that both categories live in each of us. Stereotyping the players into sides, or into agents and victims, too easily obscures the ambiguities of power, position, wisdom, possessions, and learning that torment our work and causes. We learn to think in terms of settling accounts, rather than in terms of freshly creative solutions that empower all players.

We must see the world of work within the wider context of our times. Today, our society has a new view of the earth and its creatures—including the tiny plankton of the sea and the ozone of the air. We can no longer mindlessly pollute the oceans, bulldoze the land, and poison the air. Our culture, which for centuries could glorify conquest and predation (and still models international exchanges heavily on these patterns), now looks for new ideals to serve this blue ball in space on which we all ride.

Cayce's readings plead for closer relationships to the land, both to survive a potential economic breakdown (which he saw coming to the U.S.) and to regain primal rhythms and potencies. Over and over these discourses stressed that an entire sophisticated culture, Atlantis, which was in some ways more advanced than our own, disappeared entirely from sight and memory. According to the readings, our fate—if we do not step back from worship of mindless technology and size—could be the same as that of Atlantis. In fact, many of that nation's failed but gifted leaders are now said to be reborn among us, to see whether they can make the choice better this time.

Tools and energy sources, which have decisively shaped the world of work from the Stone Age on, have been raised to what seems ultimate stature: they now hold us all hostage to nuclear annihilation. Children grow up afraid they will never reach maturity because some stupid elder will push the button that nobody dares push. Feeling impotent, the young blow their minds, which nobody can take from their reach, with drugs. They flaunt their freedom; but it is a freedom of suicide, in a world where cocreating easily yields to the more engrossing combat and devastation to be seen on any night's news. Atlantis becomes not only our parable, but our shadowy destiny.

Women have recently found dignity in the world of work that was not bestowed in the circle of the hearth. They have claimed their brains and their power, to bring a new mixture of vitality and nurturance into the marketplace, unsettling old stereotypes and hierarchies. This revolution has just begun. Few can predict all the consequences, nor name the personal crises that have already emerged in kitchens, offices, and shops, where men find not only new stature in companions, but new threats to their own one-sidedness.

Finally, the significance of ESP or psychic phenomena as a mode of work should not be overlooked. Cayce's view was that psychic processes would become widely repeated before long. If they do, attention will go not only to stretching their feats (as we now do with space travel), but to the conditions of such new creativity. We may be in the position of a society that has just invented music, or discovered electricity. Whether the new resources of psychic processes will bless us beyond measure, or simply be exploited for selfish advantage, remains to be seen.

Against such shifting panoramas, we all experience our personal crises of work and advocacy, ranging from job loss to violated rights of minorities and underdeveloped nations. Each such personal blow or impasse sets loose its own chain reaction in our lives: changing our residences and neighborhoods, contorting our budgets, replacing our autos, minimizing our health care, and limiting our friends and self-esteem. Crises in our work or social causes often lead directly to crises in personal relationships. When we are frightened that our security is gone, when we feel we will never attain the career goals we have always held, when we think that the world of often-destructive institutions cannot be changed, we look for solace and surprise to lovers, or at least to those whose grace and authority mirror what seems exiled from our souls. Often a loss in our labors develops into crises of family commitments. Or we may slowly sour, taking up each new challenge in grudging doubt.

CRISES OF WORK

Loss of Employment and Regular Income

Being fired, laid off, or replaced can sometimes be so devastating as to precipitate suicide, although a slow slide into addiction or social alienation is more common. A young black male in an urban American setting is not only vulnerable to job loss, but to the great likelihood of no work at all. A young man or woman in modern China is less likely to drift, but more likely to be nailed to whatever job he or she starts in. Increasingly, most societies are vulnerable to waves of economic depression that wash around the world as impersonally as the weather. When the crises of job loss hits, it brings a loss of self-worth and control of our lives. Our personal horror and fear can often be magnified by feelings of helplessness before impersonal social forces.

Prospects of sudden income loss and limited opportunity bedevil people who depend on child-support payments, or who work in marginal industries. American farmers face the loss of not only money, but their inheritance and their identity, as their property and tools increasingly go on the auction block. They can't sell their products, yet they see on news programs that whole nations go hungry in Africa or Latin America. The Cayce readings stressed that American farmers could and should help feed the world, but that new institutions and ethics would be required to make this possible.

Not surprisingly, Cayce's readings warned consistently that unless the employment rights of the less privileged were recognized, and unless labor received as much consideration as capital, modern America was headed for "that leveling" which could only mean revolution, with rioting and looting in the streets. Indeed, the Cayce counsel on social justice and equality, including fair treatment and opportunity for racial minorities, was far more stringent than most publishing and lecturing about him shows. His was not a purely personal ethic, focused on individual advancement, but a morality of interpenetration of responsibilities and privileges that reached every level of society.

Cayce's life readings, which offered psychological and vocational counsel for well over two thousand people, bristled with challenges to make one's work life count, and to build toward a new kind of society. Indeed, he insisted that any lifetime that did not leave the world better than one found it was a lifetime wasted and lost. The point of incarnating is service: not servitude or submission, but vital cocreating with one's fellows to make sure that each gets the opportunities needed.

Cayce also invited us to place our whole trust in God, day by day, sharing whatever blessings come along. Repeatedly he insisted that whoever did this would not find self or family "among the children of want." This was not an assurance of inevitable prosperity for those who manifested the laws of plenty. It was a much deeper promise that "the silver and gold are Mine, saith the Lord, and the cattle on a thousand hills."

The modern tendency to assign faith life to concerns of relationships, making God prisoner of hearth and school and shopping mall, finds no support in Cayce. The God he speaks about, and evidences in his astonishingly helpful readings, is a God of real estate, pollution, protest marches, banks, Wall Street, oil wells, holistic medicine, hirings and firings and inventions. No realm of human creativity, no kind of earning and building, is alien to this God, who is as much at home in the boardroom as in the bedroom. The question of whether the divine presence can be broken loose from American church and synagogue stereotypes, which often limit it to marital and family concerns, and to health concerns, must surely be one of the major issues of our times.

One consequence of alienation of the divine from employment is guilt and doubt for those who like to work. They are often told they do it only for their families, forgetting that (in the Cayce view) their model is the Creator, who spun whole worlds while fashioning families. Job loss or income loss can carry a double penalty. It means financial hardship and uncertainty; but it also means loss of productivity, of meaningful sweat, in a time when there are few social rites to mourn that kind of blow. Small sharing groups, which could be decisive resources, tend to focus on other kinds of issues—perhaps partly because men of the marketplace (often more than women) have trouble letting down their guard and sharing their feelings.

Career Changes

Because labor is so much a part of the human condition, drastic changes in work style and terms can produce crises. Even where losses of income and security are not in question, being pushed aside because of age, skin color, gender, or unfair evaluation can be devastating. When one of these blows occurs, all past failures rise up to haunt us, and we become impotent and argumentative. Changes severe enough to qualify as crises may not be as obvious as demotions or blocked promotions. They may occur anytime our fundamental competence is called into question. Transfer to a new department can do it, just as can having to learn new skills, after years in an industry now dying. When duties and roles shift, our world shifts with it; and the slide downhill hurts so much that not even strong family support may contain the pain.

Career advancement can also be unsettling, when it calls on abilities that are not well developed. People who work with the concept of reincarnation often find that they can draw up needed resources

for great shifts in work. But sometimes they discover that their misuse of talents and leadership in past lives shows up in this life as
surprising lacks that must be made up, with the inner fears and
doubts unwelcome karma brings.

Moving to a night shift, having to transfer to a new city, having
to stay in the office, having to make phone sales or lead meetings,
breaking familiar patterns—all can be costly enough to dredge up
secret self-doubts. Getting caught in office dalliances or affairs, being
trapped in unpredictable cycles of the boss's good graces or bad, suffering sexual or racial harassment, may continue for months or years,
turning part of every day into a small crisis. Some businesses run on
the rush of adrenalin. This is exhilarating, but hard on the body,
which retreats into alcohol, illness, or sexual thrills.

Work Ethics

Sometimes a business, nonprofit firm, or government agency slips
into unethical practices that damage customers, taxpayers, compet-
itors, or investors. Questions of when to blow the whistle or keep
silent, how to fight cheapness, whom to choose as allies, how to define the issues effectively, can tear up the mind and wear out the body.
Even illness can be preferable to this kind of subtle torment.

How to Deal with Work Crises

The Cayce resource can help us begin to deal with these crises of
work. Unfailingly, spiritual issues are primary. Whether for getting a
new job, choosing a career, deciding on an advancement opportunity, or struggling with work ethics, your first question must always
be this: What are my purposes, and who will truly be served? The
readings often recommend courses of action and interest, or training,
in passages that close, "This will be found beneficial spiritually, mentally, physically, and financially." The very choice of categories indicates that financial progress should be a vital dimension of any decision, and that spirituality is not to be abstracted from daily work, in
nonmaterial asceticism. It is a spirituality of cocreating in each sta-

tion and walk of life, where committee meetings, marketing strategies, assembly-line routines, labor negotiations, locating mineral deposits, promoting legislation, and handling memos are all as fitting to glorify God as cradling a baby or building a cathedral.

Many readings insist that the place to begin is to match one's own competence with purposes that are constructive for all involved. When employees find businesses deaf to such issues, and efforts to turn them around fail, the readings do not hesitate to urge job changes. On the other hand, they hold out the ideal that large corporations can operate "almost with a soul," by chosen policies and mission concepts, as well as by careful staffing and nurture of leadership.

The Cayce readings thus suggest that a work grouping can be a genuinely spiritual (though not pious) entity, and still meet the varied requirements of employees, customers, vendors, investors, and regulators. This ideal can be an exciting one in American culture. We have found this to be true in our work, having spent a quarter of a century doing business consulting with firms as large as IBM and as small as a Mom-and-Pop store. Service organizations, such as campuses and clinics and churches (where we have also done extensive consulting), can find in the Cayce perspective hearty encouragement to excellence and accountability, seeking a cocreating way of life that keeps everyone stretching toward fresh competence and fresh designs.

The recognition that God is involved at the heart of work processes themselves—not just in time off or in celebrations, or in moments of quiet before staff meetings—is crucial in keeping a spiritual dimension to the fore in work life. Tension is created in every project between task completion and person enhancement, which stresses every manager and every worker. This is a tension within the love of God, who is both Creator expressed in every worthwhile task, and parent, ever mindful of all his/her children. Tension is created between building a company culture or lore, which becomes the working scriptures of God-in-this-place; and keeping open to innovation in the same work events, where the divine is present as surpriser. This is a necessary tension within the very nature of the divine-human companionship, which honors perspective as truly as originality. In this view, to be a manager, even at a lowly level, is to be a friend of the Most High. It involves learning how to be open to guidance and transformation, and how to find the best rhythms between vigorous committed action and the openness that comes from stepping aside for reflection, meditation, and prayer.

The Cayce readings offer a fresh perspective for making work-related decisions when they speak of temperament varieties and dynamics. Here they join a major stream in Carl Jung's thought. The Cayce counsel used astrological terminology to distinguish among urges and gifts: problem-solving (Mercury); action and sensation (Mars); feelings (Venus); and intuition (Neptune and Pluto). Consideration of endowments and weaknesses in these directions of temperament, with further patterns (for example, large-minded concern for others in Jupiter, changes and cleansing in Saturn, extremes in Uranus), seemed to the Cayce trance viewpoint so crucial to effective work life that it urged their engagement in most vocational and career decisions.

Reincarnation. The Cayce readings often suggest that talents from past lives, sometimes unsuspected in the present, can turn work into adventure. Skills with fabrics or minerals or livestock, knacks of marketing and pricing, gifts of organization and negotiation, talents of analysis and invention, wisdom in financing and accounting, may be traced to past-life achievements, as they were in many of the readings. For business managers, as well as for individuals seeking their fullest expression as cocreators in the world of work, finding such beneficent karma meant watching for special resources in each person, and nurturing those that might show promise—even promise that would appear unreasonable, if reincarnation were not considered.

Dreams. Again and again, in hundreds of dream interpretations, Cayce made the case that we constantly dream of work choices. Indeed, Cayce coached two young stockbrokers to use their dreams so well that they swiftly became millionaires (although their desire to use the money for philanthropy was a major part of their success, in his view). Others were shown how every major business decision of any weight was likely to be previewed and monitored in dreams.

Working with dreams—and paying the price of personal housecleaning that may be needed to get the flow going freely—can be a major strategy for solving business crises.

Discipline and Training. The Cayce readings give high priority to competence. According to this view, individuals who want better incomes and better work opportunities are encouraged to study, train, practice, and observe worthy models. Real skill will awaken archetypes that might otherwise slumber; in so doing, they will activate helpful ESP and past karma, as well as draw outer resources. One cannot win God's favor by works, to be sure; and accumulating merit badges of skill and sacrifice can be lack of trust. Still, God is a Creator God, ever responsive to his children, who put their muscle and mouths and brains where their faith is, by cultivating excellence in their labors.

Along with competence must go a balance between cooperation and self-assertion. "The best of life is yours in cooperation with others, not in putting them down or shoving them aside," many readings counseled. At the same time, not a few were told to take risks, stick up for what they knew was right, even make mistakes rather than sit around. People who sought new jobs were counseled to "Get out the word"—don't wait to be found, or rely too much on readings and dreams. Telling associates of one's aspirations, listing oneself with employment agencies, writing letters and résumés, and making phone calls are practical strategies for beginning to take charge of a work life too often filled with unpleasant crises. In the same spirit, those who really disliked their work were warned that this was dangerous to the soul and to physical health. They should either rethink their values and ideals, to the point of actively choosing their present occupation and employment, or get out and go elsewhere.

Pregnancy and Work

Unwanted pregnancy can block education and productive labor for both the mother and the father. In the Cayce view of soul journeys, rearing children in a joyous and energetic home is itself a labor beyond any other employment—although it is not a reason to withdraw from the rich tasks of inventing and building and marketing, for a better community and a better world. Consequently, any pregnancy that does not threaten the life of the mother deserves to be taken seriously as a possible opportunity sent from God, and a possible challenge to overhaul one's priorities.

Yet the Cayce perspective is not one of tyranny of the fetus. Children should be prepared for and wanted, to have the best chance for the incoming soul. The forming body in the womb is creation's gift, to be sure; but it is not a human being until the soul enters it—and that, according to Cayce, is at the moment of birth or shortly after. In scores of cases, the readings distinguished between physical birth and soul birth, sometimes explaining that the unaccountable death of a newborn or an infant occurred because the soul that had planned to occupy the body chose to withdraw, waiting for a more suitable frame or more felicitous family circumstances. Since incoming souls were so often those that had been in the circle of the family or prized intimates in other lifetimes, they could be expected to choose their entries carefully. However, if the soul had been hovering around the pregnant mother for months, mingling its aura with those of the expectant parents, an arbitrary abortion could be as much of a blow to that soul as any other violated intimacy, and the parents would be likely to feel the grief in some inner place of consciousness.

The Cayce suggestion to parents who seek to be responsible about the relationship between procreating and creating on the job is prayer and meditation, grounded in well-thought-out ideals and paced by dreams. In dreams, one might actually encounter the face of an infant seeking to enter (as many in our practice have done)— right down to features of face and body, complexion, eyes, and gender, as well as disposition and potential talents. Unwanted pregnancy is a total challenge to one's values, not just a regrettable event. On the other hand, women who seek a child without the competence to care for it, out of a hunger for intimacy and the adulation of a dependent infant, would find this solution no solution at all, but an invitation to years of distress, requiring that they grow up swiftly into adult stature. What they visit on a child casually conceived can be expected to surface in karma of situations where their own needs would be met with only casual or irregular attention, until the soul takes account of its activities and begins to work with itself and God.

CRISES OF SOCIAL PROBLEMS

Some of life's toughest blows surely come in the arena of worthwhile causes undertaken to solve social problems. Again and again Cayce's readings singled out efforts made generously in these directions in past lives as having been times of soul gains. No matter what cause one had worked for—better education for the young, better medical care for all age levels, peace between peoples and cultures, the rights of labor, new types of communities, visions of spiritual reality, or some other avenue of invention that might lead to beauty and truth and productivity in daily life—the investment in efforts larger than personal convenience and attainment could be a source of deep companionship with God. The soul that understands this from life after life can suffer grievously when its present efforts at large-spirited causes and projects fail or are betrayed. Even those who do not recognize their larger social concerns might carry an inner current of compassion for the suffering of other groups and peoples. Cayce demonstrated this in his dream interpretation. For example, a stockbroker found himself occupied with social distress in China, where he had lived in a past life. Since most of us have lived in varied cultures and circumstances in past lives, it might be natural to have concern for those among whom we have labored and played and sung and loved.

The Four Stages of Social Change

The Cayce readings do not separate faith and politics, spirituality and justice, for these are seen as one in the eyes of God. Instead they offer an unusual perspective on worthwhile and lasting social change, which many have found helpful when their efforts at causes have foundered. Each important piece of social transformation, in this view, has to proceed through four stages: "First to the individual, then to the group, then to the classes, then to the masses." In a society half-sold to the devil of huckstering, this might seem an obvious scheme of promotion: discovering and saturating ever-widening markets. But the Cayce approach is one of cocreating, not just selling a new idea, a new institution, or even a new morality or spiritual teaching.

1. The Individual. First we must boil down the desired piece of social invention into a form that we can try out, right where we are. AA can be the model for devising a piece of social change at this level, with its twelve-step plan for individual drinkers. The effort is the same in any worthwhile social transformation: we must begin with transforming ourselves in specific activities.

2. The Group. According to the Cayce readings, once we have definite steps and procedures, it is fruitful to create groups in which to reinforce and share our discoveries. However, the task of empowering and equipping individuals cannot be left behind in favor of promoting meetings and fund raising and publications, which often absorbs groups.

3. The Classes. Vital groups generate interest among leaders of "classes"—whether these be professionals and their institutions, or those working with various reform and renewal segments of the culture, such as civil rights and feminist activities, efforts at holistic medicine, or citizen diplomacy between residents of sparring nations. For these leaders of "classes," the roles of publications, programs, and career lines can be critical. But each new recruit still needs to be shown how to work in small groups, and above all how to continue with meaningful individual effort.

4. The Masses. In time, out of the projects of these leaders in their associations and movements, and out of their creations and pilot projects, new institutional patterns will emerge. We will see new educational efforts for enculturating the young, new artifacts and architecture for implementing the change, new language and new social routines and schedules, when at last the masses take up the new pattern—still working with its individual expressions, supported by groups, and nurtured by responsible leaders.

This whole scheme might be seen as Cayce's answer to Marxism (though also incorporating elements found in dynamic Marxism, such as the cell), or as Cayce's answer to media trendiness. Cayce was trying to suggest a way of working with the Creative Forces, step by step, for lasting social transformation. To be sure, betrayal by faulty leadership may occur, as may temptations of followers to sell out to money and power, all in the name of doing good. But the person tempered by steady efforts to be a cocreator, in every walk of life, can endure these and try again, in the slow but dependable march from individual effort to mass results.

This course is slow and demanding. But many who have worked with it in various sectors of American life, whether in politics or business, medicine or education, have found it compelling and exciting, as we have seen in our professional lives and consulting.

CRISES OF ARMED ACTION

The special challenge of military service, with its variant of police work, and sometimes revolutionary or guerilla action, drew Cayce's attention. For example, one woman wanted her son excused from wartime duties, and sought a reading to find a way around them. Cayce asked her how she could pray to have her son spared, when God had not spared his, in the Christ. "For it is not all of life to live, nor all of death to die," was an expression frequently used in the readings to make the point that quality of life is more significant than mere duration—just as death is an interruption, but not an ending. In a longer view, which incorporates reincarnation, love might require risking all.

Cayce risked his own existence in his trances, which took him into altered states that at times clearly threatened his life. Following this example, people who love freedom and hate tyranny and bigotry and hunger and disease might take very large risks, trusting themselves to a merciful God. If their lives are taken, then further opportunities for growth and service will follow in another existence. If their lives are spared, then they have cause not only for gratitude, but for redoubled responsibility—for their own lives and the lost lives of their fellows.

International peace was such a high priority in these readings as to be made the basis for the destiny of America, which would lose its leadership in the family of nations if it did not make every effort in that direction. The readings were not categorically pacifist, however, although they gave support to those who took such a stance. Instead, the Cayce resource put the burden of decision on each individual. When the issue was no longer active service, but postwar recovery from military patterns of violence that twisted and confused the soul, the readings offered patient encouragement toward forgiveness.

CRISES OF BROKEN DREAMS

Far less dramatic than risking organs and limbs in military action, yet devastating to many, is the crisis that results from blasted dreams. If indeed souls are "corpuscles in the body of God" and inclined to productive creativity because of the very nature of their Creator, then not being allowed to reach one's fullest potential, or indeed to be degraded in one's round of life, can create victims as surely as can guns and bombs. Those who reach for education and employment, for friendship and artistry and adventure, but find their way blocked by barriers of race or gender or age or lack of experience, can suffer as much as those visited by death loss. But the grieving is often hidden in our society, or obscured by the cries of indignant spokespeople who are discounted as pushing special interests. Yet the effects of shock after shock in rejection contain all the elements of frightening pain and doubt, requiring fresh places to begin in the struggle with work crises.

The Cayce readings do not typically counsel acceptance of injustice without struggle, advising people that if their environs are unsatisfactory, they should set to work with others to change them, especially when the patterns injure many. Means and ends must match, in such struggles, for one could seem to gain the whole world yet lose one's soul and have to be reborn to reclaim it. Always ideals and purposes must govern, even while one struggles with campaigns, strategies, recruiting, funding, rallies, and marches.

In this view, prayer is an important dimension of social change, for God will save a whole city (as in biblical times) or a firm or a social movement, because of the prayers of a few righteous women and men, living what they pray. Those who find this hard to imagine should recall how small groups and social currents—such as the Essenes in New Testament times, the growing democracy of the American colonies, and the nonviolent teachings of Gandhi—could have great social impact because they embodied a profound archetypal design, which could surface swiftly in times of turmoil.

In counseling how to take on social abuses, the readings drew on a biblical phrase to urge, "Be angry but sin not." Some wrongs deserve passionate and blazing outrage, but not as vehicles for ego, either as vengeance or as self-pity. Many who have misused anger and violence in other lives will find it difficult to carry off sustained passion against tyranny or belittling, preferring to back off rather than risk exploding with rage that might destroy someone or embarrass themselves. "One without a temper isn't worth much," advises this counsel. But often the readings add, "One who doesn't control it is worth less."

From the perspective of reincarnation, unjust discrimination carries a quiet warning, requiring the sufferer to ask, "Have I ever done this to others? Am I capable of it, somewhere in my life?" Often there will be an echo from within—perhaps from behavior in the family circle, or from violated lovers or friendships—to suggest that karma is at work in the suffering created by broken dreams. Such karma is not meant to be borne with subservient resignation. But the one who has some hint that constriction in the present might mirror unworthiness in the soul has to choose to see all sides of a painful controversy, and to offer the same compassion to others as one would desire for one's own sins. Thus praying for enemies and tormentors, in all sincerity, is as real to the Cayce readings as it is in the New Testament. Such prayer, matched by compassion as great as the firmness of resistance to abuse, can turn one's inner ambiguities around, and free the stern workings of karma to become the gentle workings of grace.

CRISES OF FINANCIAL CATASTROPHE

In financial calamity, circumstances overwhelm our resources and earning potentials. The sudden events may arrive from nature, whether from microbes or viruses in the body, or collapse of the body into aging or senility. They may come from storms or floods, fires or tornadoes. They may come in shattering auto accidents or falls, or in criminal attacks.

Just as devastating are sudden turns of affairs in daily commerce. A bank note may be called in, and all of one's resources are suddenly wiped out. Bankruptcy may be forced on us, or a lawsuit pressed, such that all our assets become hostage to outrageous fortune. If the calamity can clearly be traced to our own mistakes in judgment (whether in steering a car or steering a business, or in failure to insure properly or to employ wise counsel), then our grief and dismay is compounded with shame and guilt—already aroused by a desperate sense of inadequacy from a storm of circumstance. Looking around in agony, we find people on every side who count on us, needing hospital care that never seems to end, or just needing food, clothing, and dignity. Or we see creditors who have trusted us and now must be stalled or unwillingly defrauded. In such crises, the heart fails, the will crumbles, and we wonder if the very universe is against us. All of our feelings of unworthiness come to the fore, compounded by furtive temptations to escape it all in an affair, running away, or even suicide.

Where can we even begin in manifest financial calamity? Cayce knew the face of this dragon well, after fires repeatedly destroyed his photographic studios—once when they were filled with precious, uninsured paintings. As always, beginning again requires turning to God in prayer and reflection. After his oil well failures, Cayce spent months away from home lecturing, often alone in his hotel room and studying his Bible, thinking out his life, and praying and meditating.

Slowly guidance came as to what to take up next, whom to seek out, where to begin. He started over. Almost at once an entirely new kind of reading emerged from his talent: the life readings that traced reincarnation and karma in individual tapestries. His readings linked his determination to carry on to the emergence of this entirely new kind of counsel. In this view, nothing succeeds like a first-class failure, when one puts everything possible into it.

In calamities that result from acts of nature, or the catastrophes of illness, or the blind maelstroms of war, the process is similar. Those who put their whole trust in God, and are willing to take one step at a time—starting right where they are, with whatever pitiful-seeming resources—will be met by fresh opportunities.

When arbitrary legal action wipes out our assets, the Cayce counsel is to stand up for our rights, yet avoid pointless hostilities. Forgiving and releasing, when a chapter of our life is over, has more merit than getting tangled up in everlasting regrets and recriminations. So when Cayce was sued to recover the hospital that had been built for him, by its young backers hard pressed by the Depression, he simply gave it back—although it nearly broke his heart to lose it, as well as to watch it be made into a hotel and eventually a nightclub. In its place, life brought him again a new kind of reading, which focused on small groups. This may prove to be his most valuable contribution of all, in its larger social applications.

Whatever the blow that upsets our aspirations for meaningful work, for needed social change, for family stability and security, the perspectives in the Cayce readings are similar. All hardships can be opportunities for the greatest adventure of all: setting forth into the seas of God, where a wind from any direction only pushes the sail and shoots the trembling craft on, toward destinations full of surprises to be shared with others, not for months or for years, but for lifetimes ahead.

10

Crises of Colliding with Oneself

SOME CRISES COME FROM within ourselves: our own illness, runaway emotions, cravings, crimes, and betrayals of principle and trust. We may feel so done in by the failure within us—of body, mind, or spirit—that we hardly want to go on.

Social rituals can help see us through such crises as illness, injury, dying, and aging. These command the attention of those who love us, at least initially. But when we fail ourselves by poor judgment or impulsiveness, the social rituals may be punitive. Our loneliness is made worse because those around us secretly dread that their own weaknesses might undo them in turn. Consciously or not, they try to avoid us.

The consequences of such major confrontations with ourselves touch our entire lives. Inevitably we look back over our days, to see where we lost our way or whether the good we have done might cover up our lacks. Men who have been taught not to weep or show vulnerable feelings may have a hard time of it. But men are allowed to rage and drink, and get it out that way. Women often find society expects them to confront their private horrors with tears and illness, when they would rather destroy something in their agony. Trapped by the ultimate trapper, ourselves, we all want to lash out when we crash into our own beings, and we must use care not to wound those around us.

LOSING TRUST IN GOD

Perhaps the worst personal crisis is the feeling that we have let our relation with God shrivel, until it is a dried little umbilicus, connecting us to nothing. If there is a God, we feel we have lost all our credit, so that it is too late now to open an account. We not only skipped the proper services, read few proper scriptures, and neglected proper sharing with the needy, but we let the whole matter slide. God got overlooked, in the dash to the commuter train. God got filed with important papers, to be opened at our demise.

The consequence of such actions or inactions can be hollow desolation. Final trust is missing to help us face our own death, desertion, or double dealing. What can we do in the face of this ultimate loss?

The Cayce readings tell us that it is never too late. God's total acceptance is instantaneous, if we seek it without dodge or bargaining. Whatever we would offer to a lost child—and more—is there for us without hesitation, from the One that loves us most intimately of all. Such acceptance is not a free pass to go wandering again, testing the limits like a rebellious child. It is not a promise that nothing will come of our neglect or manipulation or cruelty—for the universe is designed to educate us, in all the ways that we have called karma. The acceptance means that we can take on the growing and changing that must follow, without the crushing guilt and sense of distance from the holy that was there only yesterday. Even when the crisis is the horror of having taken another's life, the promise still holds: God does not execute us, whatever the courts may do. As the readings insist, "He hath not willed that any soul should perish, but hath with every temptation—or trial—provided a means of escape." The escape offered is not escape from consequences, but escape from stupefying loneliness. What we must take on now will be bearable, because God carries the other end of our load.

Further, the Cayce readings suggest that we cannot get into more trouble than we can get out of, with God's help. In this view, it is our imagination and will that got us to such a sorry state in the first place, and our drive that kept us there. When we are at last utterly stuck, the same imagination can think up fresh beginnings, the same will can keep our resolve clean and generous, the same drive can carry us through to sunlight. The Cayce readings insist that God will not allow us to be tested more than we can bear—partly because the resources we use to take apart our lives are the same resources that can pull them together.

These claims cannot be demonstrated like mathematical equations. They can only be lived out, one day at a time. We can tell you that in our counseling practice, we have repeatedly seen that gambling on the Cayce perspective can bring the release of fear, the quiet creativity, and the decency and dignity that Cayce predicted.

TERMINAL ILLNESS OR MENTAL ILLNESS

Incapacitating or terminal illness can defeat all our best intentions. Waking up speechless and motionless after a stroke, lying still in numbed fright with tubes and oxygen after a heart attack, staring in disbelief at crushed or missing limbs after an auto accident—such events can seem more difficult than dying. If we know we must die, then we can take a deep breath and step across to a new life. But if we must live, yet hardly live, then it is not only blood that must be transfused, but the courage to go on.

In the Cayce view, God is in charge of all rescue—when asked. Strangers in white coats are sent to the hospital bed from realms unknown, as the psyche reenacts all the bonding of an infant with its life-giving mother. We will long remember the doctors and nurses and attendants, because they came as mercy itself. Certain friends and relatives whom we thought only polite will turn out to have true compassion. They astonish us with their faithfulness, when we can offer nothing in return but a weak smile.

As students of "primitive" tribes have noted, great suffering makes us all shamans. It strips off our masks at the same time it activates our centers. With a little strength here and there, we can know—even in a sickbed—when to encourage a busy mother to rest, a father to play with his youngsters, either parent to strike out for new employment, or the whole family to go fishing or move to a new school district. For final events bring final truths. Those who come to cheer us in a loss of a kidney, a mastectomy, or the beginnings of a long battle with cancer find themselves standing at the foot of the bed in silence: for they see on the pillow a face utterly unpretending, and a smile and calm assurance, even in great pain, that flow straight from the soul. If we choose to put our trust in God, we are given a secret dignity and wisdom that others will cherish for longer than we guess.

Mental illness may make us weep or rage or withdraw in chilling despair, uncertain of which way is up or who is on our side. Yet the psyche, which longs for God, may contrive out of even its bizarre fantasies and defenses little bits of a world of ultimates. Others may not always be able to enter that world with us; but as Anton Boisen and others have suggested, and our own clinical experience has shown, what the mind creates when it spins on itself is often surprisingly ennobling, even in its baffling strangeness. Jung demonstrated repeatedly how much archetypal imagery there was in the refrains or rituals of the psychotic, so that one can suggest with Cayce that the mind undone is not ripped away from the treasures of the soul.

Cayce's approach to fresh beginnings for serious mental illness almost always began with the body. He saw incoordination of the two great nervous systems—cerebrospinal and autonomic—as so important that he affirmed that as many as 80 percent of those in mental hospitals (in his day) could be cured with proper osteopathic care. Enough cases piled up in his files to give the claims some credence. At the same time, he offered his version of therapeutic community, calling for sponsorship of the one sorely troubled. Treatment measures were as rich as those for illnesses of the body. But the first strategies were always compassion and prayer, with the caretakers reminded that the roles might have been reversed in a prior life, or might yet be in a later existence. Many times Cayce indicated that mental illness comes as opportunity for soul growth to all concerned.

AGING

As we age we seem to lose parts of ourselves—hearing, sight, and teeth begin to go; sleep takes on different patterns. We cannot lift or leap as once we might; and sex becomes problematic. We grope around a room for our glasses, and then grope for our memory, dismayed to have something so intimate fail us. Joints move with creaks or shooting pain; even getting out of a car is ungainly. We may feel that we are a burden on a world that once was fully ours. When the aging begins with the death of a loved partner, or of children we thought would long outlast us, then so much is gone that we wonder who it is that answers to our name.

Cayce's strategy for aging is to begin helping those around us who are worse off than we are: more infirm, younger, poorer, less educated, more lonely—and someone always appears if we look. Sponsorship is now not merely an adventure, but high privilege. Age brings with it dignity, unless we soil it with whining and pettiness. We may use a glance, a backrub, a time of thoughtful listening as the scepter of our royal selfhood to confirm stature in others.

Even those whose final years are relatively easy are not spared other crises. Unless channels have been carved for service, the life force that has flowed so freely for years slows to a trickle. The Cayce counsel is to plan ahead for the flow of vital energies to run down new streambeds—some of them play, and some sacrifice for others. Since much karma has been met and mastered by this time, there is reason to teach or advise the younger—when they ask for it! In so doing, those in full season of their days may not only keep their wits and their health, but code many levels of the psyche for the wisdom that the soul will carry into the next life. This wisdom will be nearer the surface than if the last years are spent in aimless rituals.

We can always feed our hunger for music or the arts, even if we have to use a mouth organ instead of a piano. The soul is ever greater than its circumstances, if it takes what it has and offers it freely to others. "We only keep what we give away," is the repeated Cayce counsel. This is not merely rhetorical encouragement, but is intended to suggest that we *can* take with us what is worth taking. When the ultimate retirement comes, into a region much farther than Florida or Arizona, we slip out of the body into a realm where the light is lovelier than any sunlight—when we seek it out. In the Cayce view, the psyche prepares for the death transition in dreams, presenting adventures of travel, happy weddings, gracious garments—for the soul knows where it has often been before, and remembers that death is no threat, but only the visit of a gentle friend. Death in this view should ultimately be no crisis.

EXCESSES

The crises of facing our personal excesses often carry the odor of moral failure. Most of us bump into ourselves in runaway emotions at some time: raging, blaming, self-pity, ill-tempered sexuality. Or we take a turn at outsize appetites, for food or drink or drugs or danger. There is also the self-damage in which we withdraw, hold back, or otherwise cheat life as truly as if we robbed it impulsively. Jung has suggested (with a bit of whimsy, but also seriousness) that the human race can be divided into those who hold back, only to regret their miserliness of feelings and relationships, and those who leap in, but must later rue their impulsiveness. All too often the savers and the leapers marry each other, or form business partnerships, leading to intricate misunderstandings and regrets as well as to growth.

Freud has developed his own scheme of styles of being human and getting stuck, which psychiatrist Karen Horney suggested could be styles of "toward" (oral, in excesses of gullibility and ingesting opinions or relationships without digesting); "away" (anal, with excesses of withholding and compulsive orderliness); "against" (phallic, with excesses of overcompetitiveness and showing off); and "with" (genital, where excesses yield to cocreating potency). The Cayce readings also offer hints of these patterns, in interpretations of dreams, and in medical-psychological counsel to the wounded. Each of us can find our own strengths and weaknesses. Presumably these are not begun in childhood alone, in the Cayce view, but started in one or more prior lives. But the challenge presented in the readings is not to find a place in a typology or set of labels. It is to take responsibility for our lives, while paradoxically yielding them to God at the same time, toward that cocreating that carries the greatest human joy.

As a protection against excesses, the Cayce readings uniformly advise self-study and self-analysis: "Step aside and watch self go by"; and "If you don't like what you see, change it." To change negative attitudes, the readings say simply, "Begin, get started!" A kind of behavior-modification strategy is often evident in such encouragement. What one does, a little bit at a time, can bring its own quick reinforcement, and provide momentum toward new behaviors. Cayce did not advise phoniness, or mere manipulation of behavior. In keeping with his view of the suggestibility of the psyche, he did not hesitate to suggest that action toward behaviors consonant with chosen ideals would eventually tame many a recalcitrant attitude. He insisted that just as humans could bring the horse under such training that it would enjoy galloping to the next worthy command, so the psyche itself could and should be tamed by larger purpose infused with the divine will. "He that conquereth self doeth more than he that taketh a city."

When we are reeling under the impact of personal crisis, counsel to conquer self may seem outrageous. Often the goal is just to find a workable self for the next day and the next night. But the Cayce readings consistently present the longer view as worthy of attention. In this view, no promise is more often affirmed than that we do not need to invent our lives from scratch. One named the Christ has done it all before, and knows the way. When asked, this one (whom Cayce called "the Elder Brother," to suggest his closeness to the human condition) would be there to help, working quietly to magnify helpful archetypes that are the treasures of the soul in its long journey.

Our destiny lands us all in the fiery furnace, by karma or some other mystery of our large becoming. Shock and weeping yield at last to wonder, when we see that flames of pain have destroyed our often self-imposed bonds. Shall we then crawl back into our prisoners' bunks, sleeping off the nightmares of our troubled days? Or shall we wake up to full effort that rights the wrongs on every side, and signals the time for unguessed adventure into God? The choice is up to each of us. We must make our own decisions and take our own risks, for "Affairs are now soul-size."

SELECTED
BIBLIOGRAPHY

Anonymous. *A Search for God, Books I and II*. Virginia Beach, VA: A.R.E. Press, 1942, 1945.

Bridges, William. *Transitions*. Reading, MA: Addison-Wesley, 1980.

Think on These Things: Selections from the Edgar Cayce Readings. Virginia Beach, VA: A.R.E. Press, 1981.

Cayce, Edgar. *What I Believe*. Virginia Beach, VA: A.R.E. Press, 1946.

Cayce, Hugh Lynn. *Faces of Fear*. San Francisco: Harper & Row, 1980.

———. *Venture Inward*. San Francisco: Harper & Row, 1964.

Colgrove, Melba, Harold H. Bloomfield, and Peter McWilliams. *How to Survive the Loss of a Love*. New York: Bantam Books, 1976.

Dass, Ram, and Paul Gorman. *How Can I Help?* New York: Knopf, 1987.

Drummond, Richard. *Unto the Churches*. Virginia Beach, VA: A.R.E. Press, 1978.

Ferguson, Marilyn. *The Aquarian Conspiracy*. Los Angeles: Tarcher, 1980.

Fry, Christopher. *A Sleep of Prisoners* in *Three Plays*. New York: Oxford University Press, 1951.

Goodman, Ellen. *Turning Points*. New York: Fawcett Crest, 1979.

Hall, Calvin S., and Vernon Nordby. *A Primer of Jungian Psychology*. New York: New American Library, 1973.

Hyatt, Carole, and Linda Gottlieb. *When Smart People Fail*. New York: Penguin, 1987.

Jung, C. G. *Answer to Job*. Princeton: Princeton University Press, 1969.

———. *Man and His Symbols*. New York: Doubleday, 1964.

———. *Two Essays in Analytical Psychology*. Princeton: Princeton University Press, 1972.

Keen, Sam. *The Passionate Life*. San Francisco: Harper & Row, 1983.

Kübler-Ross, Elisabeth. *AIDS: The Ultimate Challenge*. New York: Macmillan, 1987.

———. *On Death and Dying*. New York: Macmillan, 1969.

Kushner, Harold S. *When Bad Things Happen to Good People*. New York: Avon, 1981.

Leonard, Linda S. *The Wounded Woman*. Boston: Shambhala, 1985.

McGarey, William A. *Healing Miracles: Using Your Body Energies*. San Francisco: Harper & Row, 1988.

McGarey, William, and Gladys McGarey. *There Will Your Heart Be Also*. New York: Bantam Books, 1988.

Peck, M. Scott. *The Different Drum*. New York: Simon and Schuster, 1987.

———. *People of the Lie*. New York: Simon and Schuster, 1983.

———. *The Road Less Traveled*. New York: Simon and Schuster, 1978.

Reed, Henry. *Awakening Your Psychic Powers*. San Francisco: Harper & Row, 1988.

Schuller, Robert H. *Tough Times Never Last, But Tough People Do*. New York: Bantam Books, 1984.

Sheehy, Gail. *Passages*. New York: Bantam Books, 1976.

Stearns, Ann Kaiser. *Living Through Personal Crisis*. New York: Ballantine Books, 1985.

Tart, Charles. *Psi*. New York: Dutton, 1977.

Thurston, Mark A. *How to Interpret Your Dreams*. Virginia Beach, VA: A.R.E. Press, 1978.

———. *Paradox of Power*. Virginia Beach, VA: A.R.E. Press, 1987.

———. *Understand and Develop Your ESP*. Virginia Beach, VA: A.R.E. Press, 1977.

Turner, Victor. *The Ritual Process*. Ithaca: Cornell University Press, 1969.

Van der Post, Laurens. *Jung and the Story of Our Time*. New York: Random House, 1975.

Whitmont, Edward. *The Symbolic Quest*. Princeton: Princeton University Press, 1978.

INDEX

ABOUT THE AUTHORS

Harmon Hartzell Bro, Ph.D., brings to the subject of life crises more than three decades as a pastoral counselor and psychotherapist, using a Jungian perspective. In addition, he draws on his unique experience as the only living professional person who worked closely with Edgar Cayce, observing six hundred of his trance discourses. He has served on the staff of teaching hospitals in the Philadelphia and Chicago areas, and is a contributor to the *Encyclopaedia Britannica*. His books include a study of Martin Buber's thought, a biography of Cayce, and six books on Cayce's concepts, including the widely read and translated *Edgar Cayce on Dreams*. As a specialist in the psychology of religion, he has been a teaching fellow at Harvard, held a chair at Syracuse University, and been a graduate dean at Drake University. Currently he is a visiting scholar at Harvard, and is co-director of Pilgrim Institute, founded in the Boston area in 1974. He appears frequently on television and has lectured on more than forty campuses.

June Avis Bro, D. Min., is a pastoral counselor with a Jungian orientation who has specialized in the growth journeys of women, both in her private practice and in the lecturing and workshops that have taken her across the United States and Canada for decades. She has used Cayce's concepts not only in her doctoral studies but in staff positions at a hospital crisis center, a halfway house for addicts, and a therapeutic farm for young adult psychotics, as well as in pastoral leadership of Philadelphia and Chicago churches. She has been a research assistant at Harvard and taught at half a dozen campuses, while rearing five children. Currently she is codirector of Pilgrim Institute, engaged in research on women's spirituality and in leading overseas study tours to the Near East and China.

EDGAR CAYCE'S
WISDOM FOR THE NEW AGE

More information from the Edgar Cayce readings is available to you on hundreds of topics from astrology and arthritis to universal laws and world affairs, because Cayce's friends established an organization, the Association for Research and Enlightenment (A.R.E.), to facilitate his readings and make the information available for research.

Today over 75,000 members of the A.R.E. receive the bimonthly magazine *Venture Inward*, which contains articles on dream interpretation, past lives, health and diet tips, psychic archaeology, and psi research, as well as book reviews and interviews with leaders and authors in the metaphysical field. Members also receive extracts of medical and nonmedical readings and may do their own research in all of the over fourteen thousand readings that Edgar Cayce gave during his lifetime.

To receive more information about the association that continues to research and make available information on subjects in the Edgar Cayce readings, please write A.R.E., Dept. M13, P.O. Box 595, Virginia Beach, VA 23451, or call (804) 428–3588. The A.R.E. will be happy to send you a packet of materials describing its current activities.